HEY, WAIT...

by jason

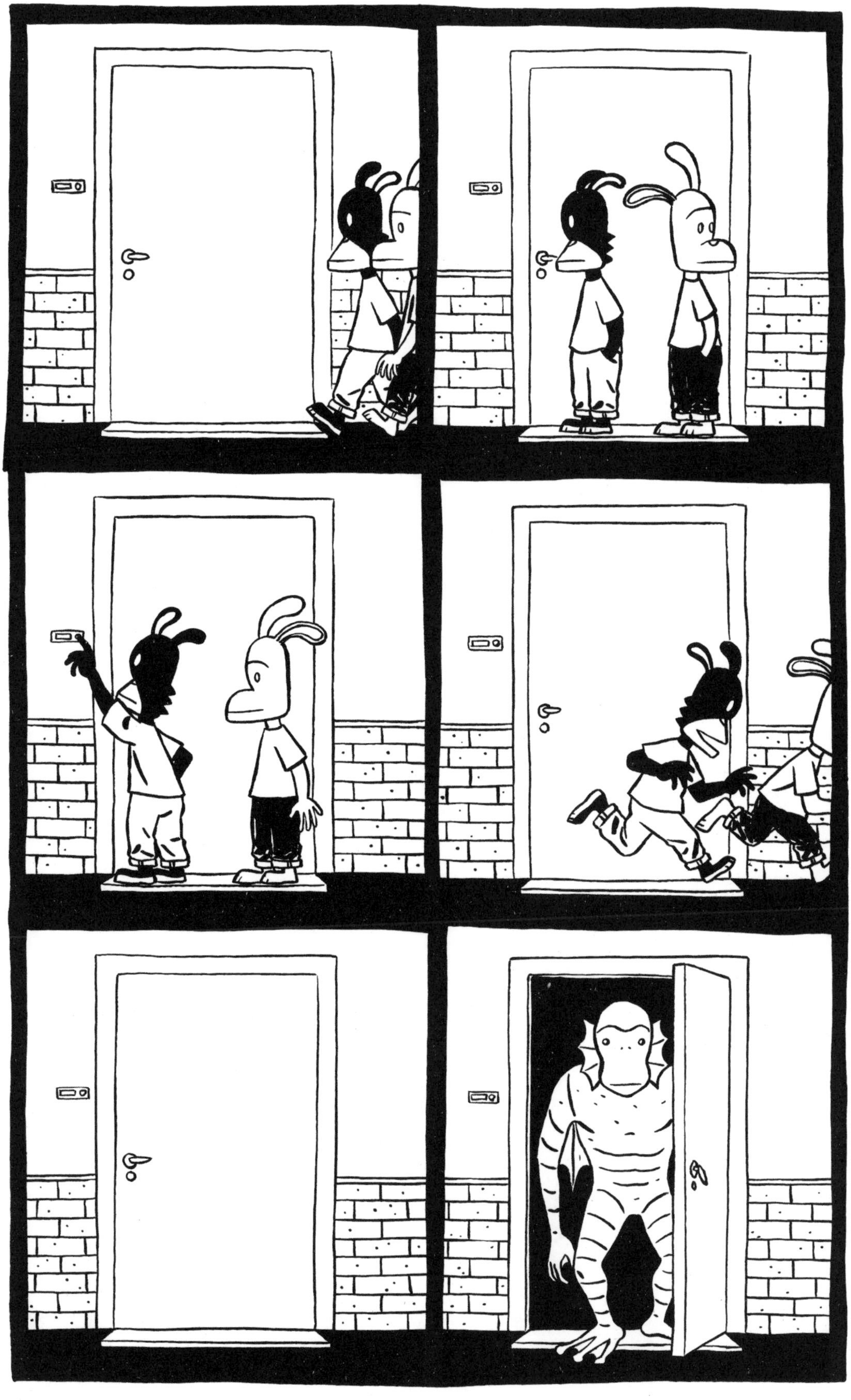

FANTAGRAPHICS BOOKS

7563 Lake City Way NE
Seattle WA 98115

Edited and translated (from the Norwegian) by Kim Thompson
Designed by Jason
Production by Peppy White and Paul Baresh
Published by Gary Groth and Kim Thompson

Special thanks to Erik Falk of Jippi Forlag and Daniel Pellegrino of Atrabile

To receive a free catalog of cool comics, call 1-800-657-1100 or write us at Fantagraphics Books,
7563 Lake City Way NE, Seattle, WA 98115; you can also visit the Fantagraphics website at www.fantagraphics.com!

Visit the website for Jippi Forlag, where Jason's work appeared initially, at www.jippicomics.com!

First printing: September 2001

ISBN: 0-56097-463-X

Printed in Canada

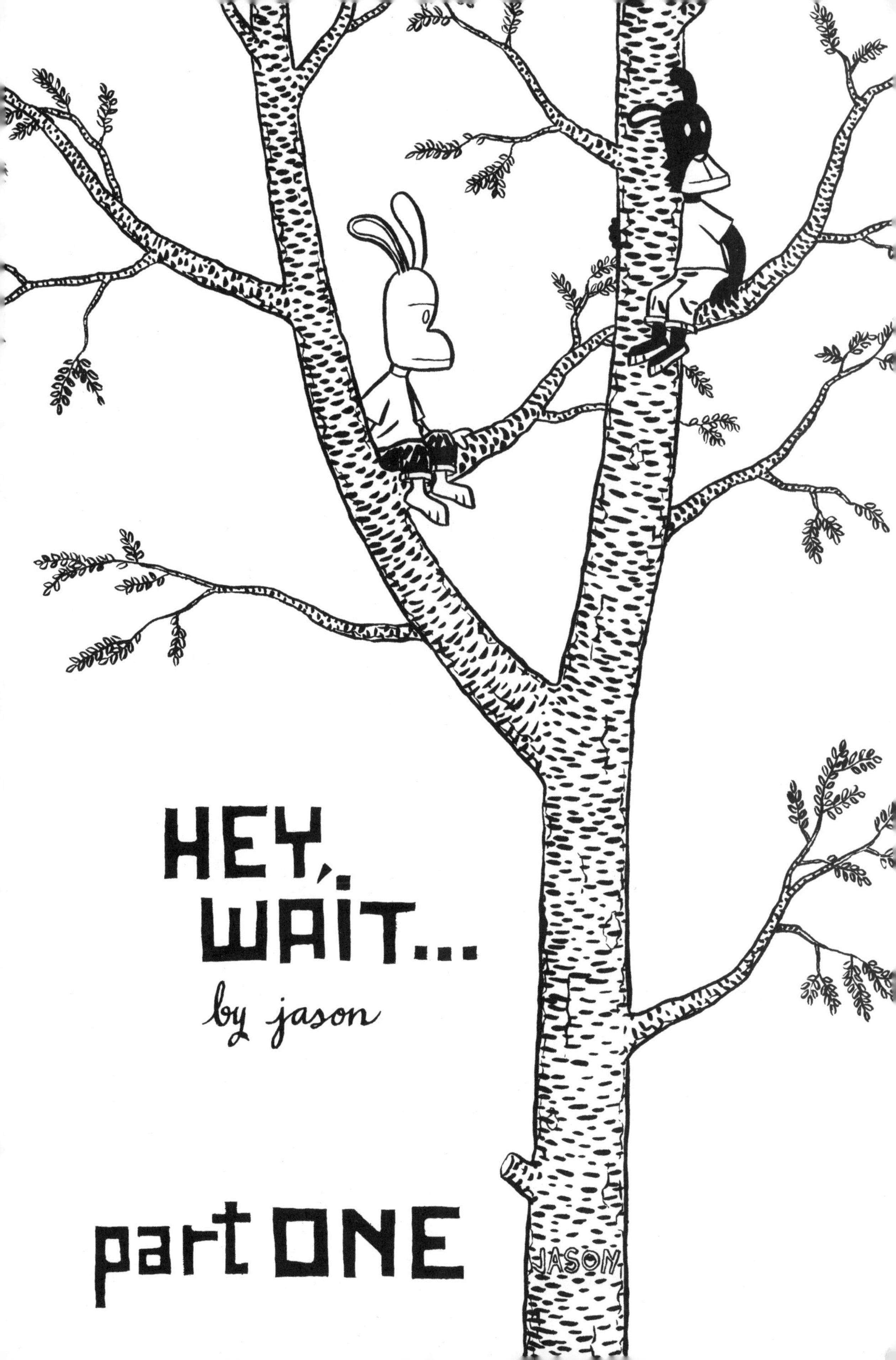
JASON

HEY, WAIT...

by jason

part ONE

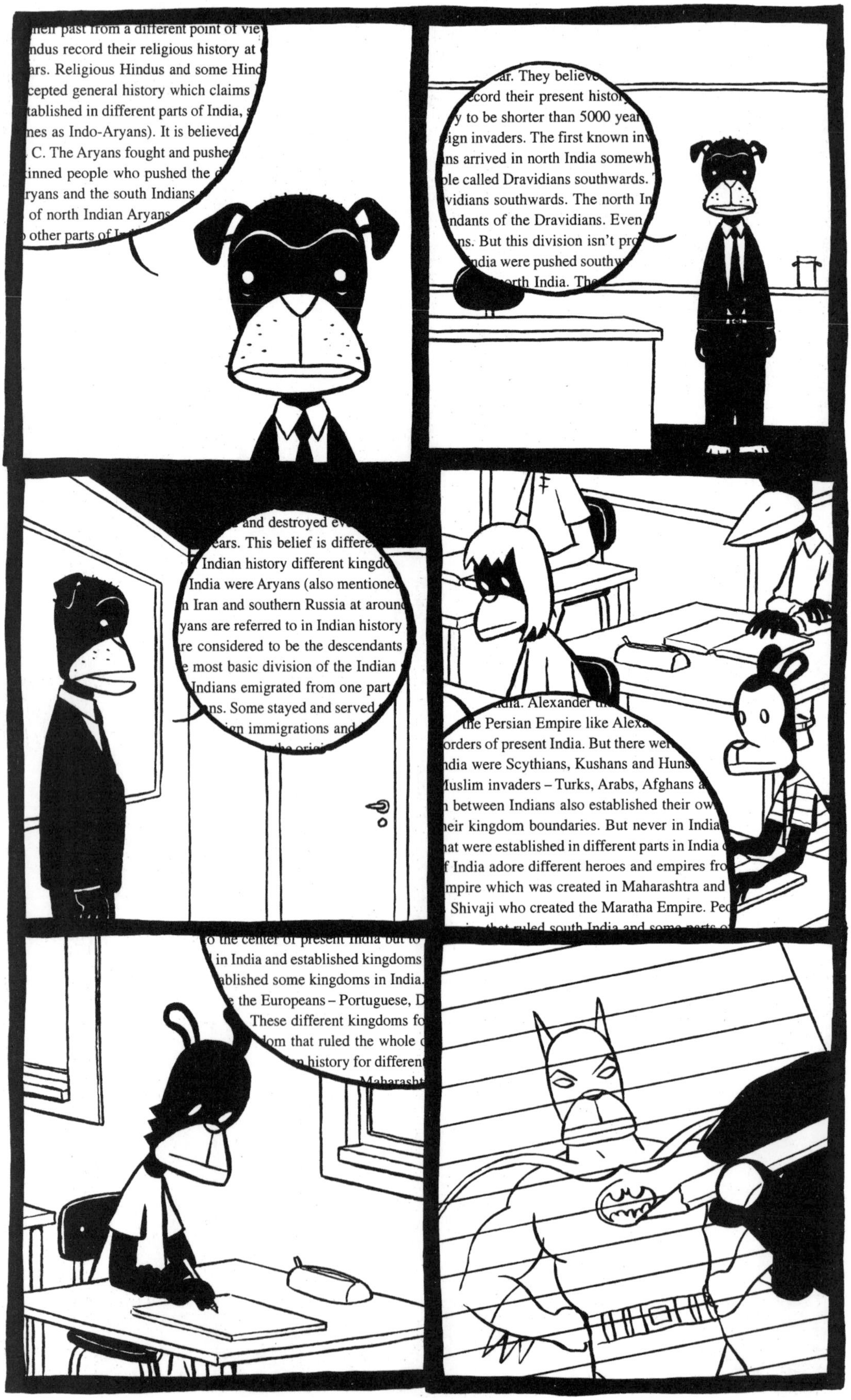
ndus record their religious history at
ars. Religious Hindus and some Hind
cepted general history which claims
tablished in different parts of India,
nes as Indo-Aryans). It is believed
C. The Aryans fought and pushe
kinned people who pushed the
ryans and the south Indians
of north Indian Aryans
other parts of
ar. They believe
ecord their present histor
y to be shorter than 5000 yea
ign invaders. The first known in
ns arrived in north India somewh
ple called Dravidians southwards.
vidians southwards. The north In
ndants of the Dravidians. Even
ns. But this division isn't pr
ndia were pushed southw
rth India. Th
and destroyed ev
ears. This belief is differe
Indian history different kingd
India were Aryans (also mentione
Iran and southern Russia at aroun
ryans are referred to in Indian history
re considered to be the descendants
most basic division of the Indian
Indians emigrated from one part
ns. Some stayed and served
ign immigrations and
dia. Alexander
the Persian Empire like Alexa
orders of present India. But there we
ndia were Scythians, Kushans and Huns
Muslim invaders – Turks, Arabs, Afghans
between Indians also established their ow
eir kingdom boundaries. But never in India
at were established in different parts in India
India adore different heroes and empires fro
mpire which was created in Maharashtra and
Shivaji who created the Maratha Empire. Pe
in India and established kingdoms
blished some kingdoms in India.
the Europeans – Portuguese, D
These different kingdoms fo
dom that ruled the whole
history for different

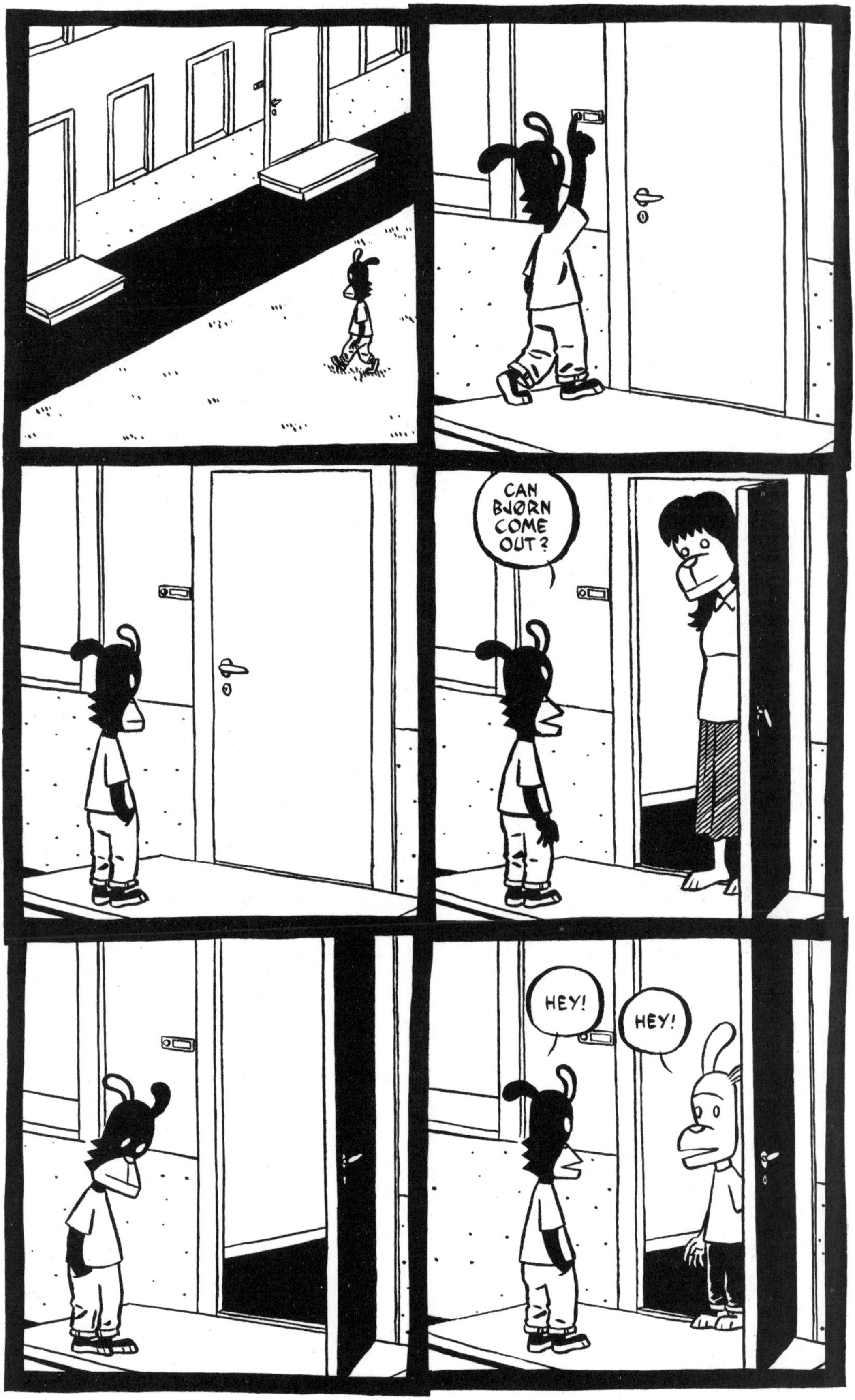
CAN BJØRN COME OUT?
HEY!
HEY!

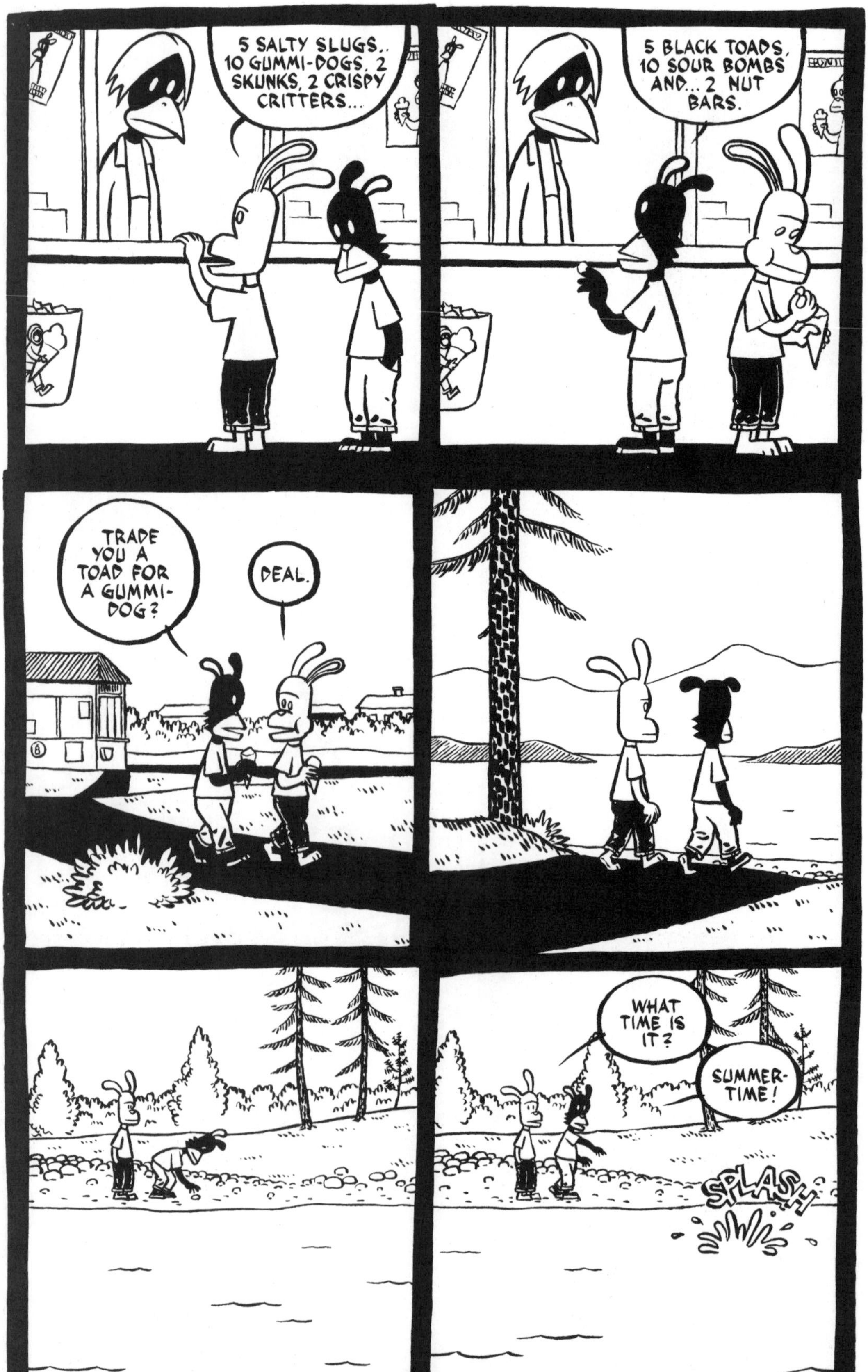
5 SALTY SLUGS.. 10 GUMMI-DOGS, 2 SKUNKS, 2 CRISPY CRITTERS...
5 BLACK TOADS, 10 SOUR BOMBS AND... 2 NUT BARS.
TRADE YOU A TOAD FOR A GUMMI-DOG?
DEAL.
WHAT TIME IS IT?
SUMMER-TIME!
SPLASH

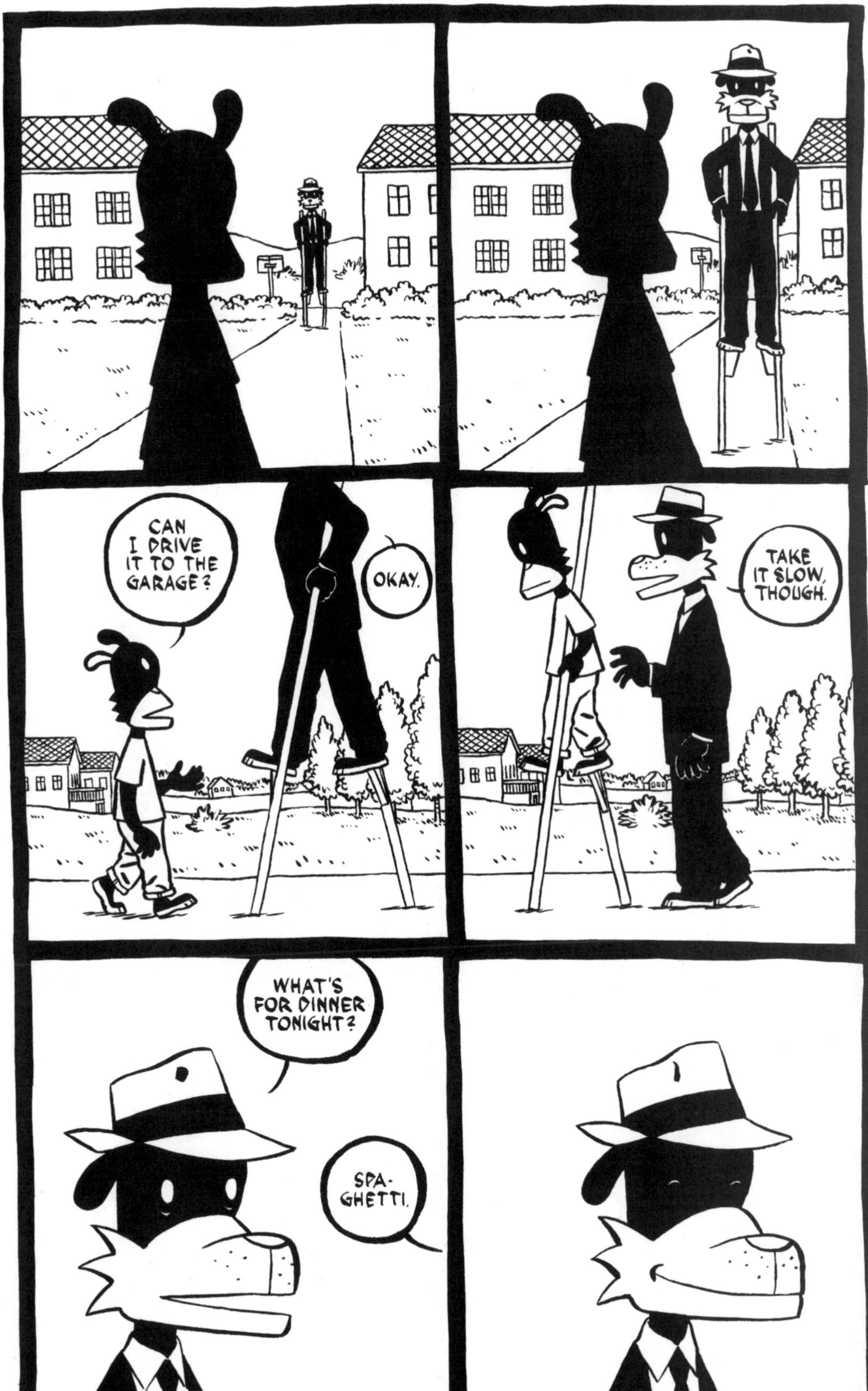
CAN I DRIVE IT TO THE GARAGE?
OKAY.
TAKE IT SLOW, THOUGH.
WHAT'S FOR DINNER TONIGHT?
SPA-GHETTI.

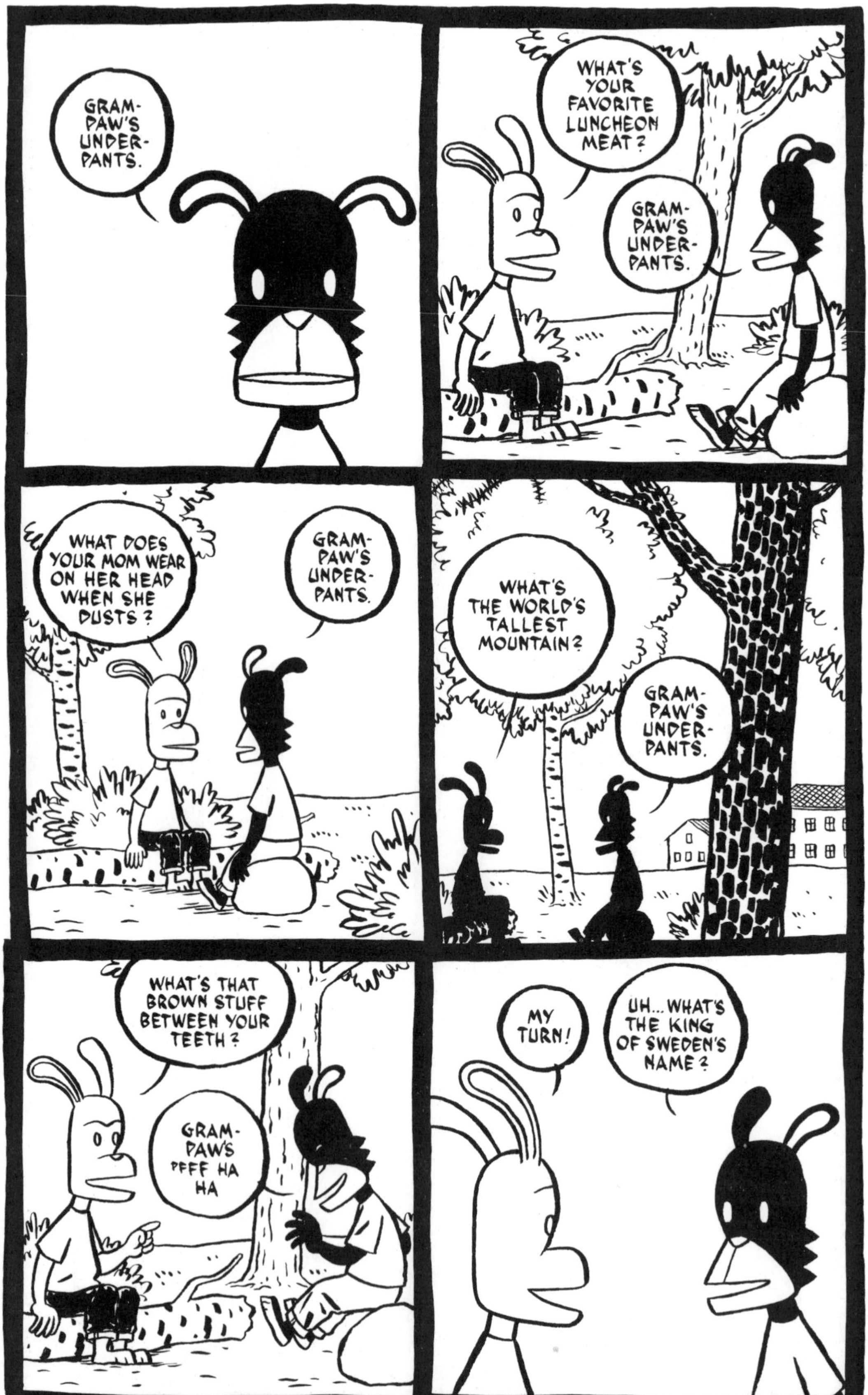
GRAM-PAW'S UNDER-PANTS.
WHAT'S YOUR FAVORITE LUNCHEON MEAT?
GRAM-PAW'S UNDER-PANTS.
WHAT DOES YOUR MOM WEAR ON HER HEAD WHEN SHE DUSTS?
GRAM-PAW'S UNDER-PANTS.
WHAT'S THE WORLD'S TALLEST MOUNTAIN?
GRAM-PAW'S UNDER-PANTS.
WHAT'S THAT BROWN STUFF BETWEEN YOUR TEETH?
GRAM-PAWS PFFF HA HA
MY TURN!
UH... WHAT'S THE KING OF SWEDEN'S NAME?

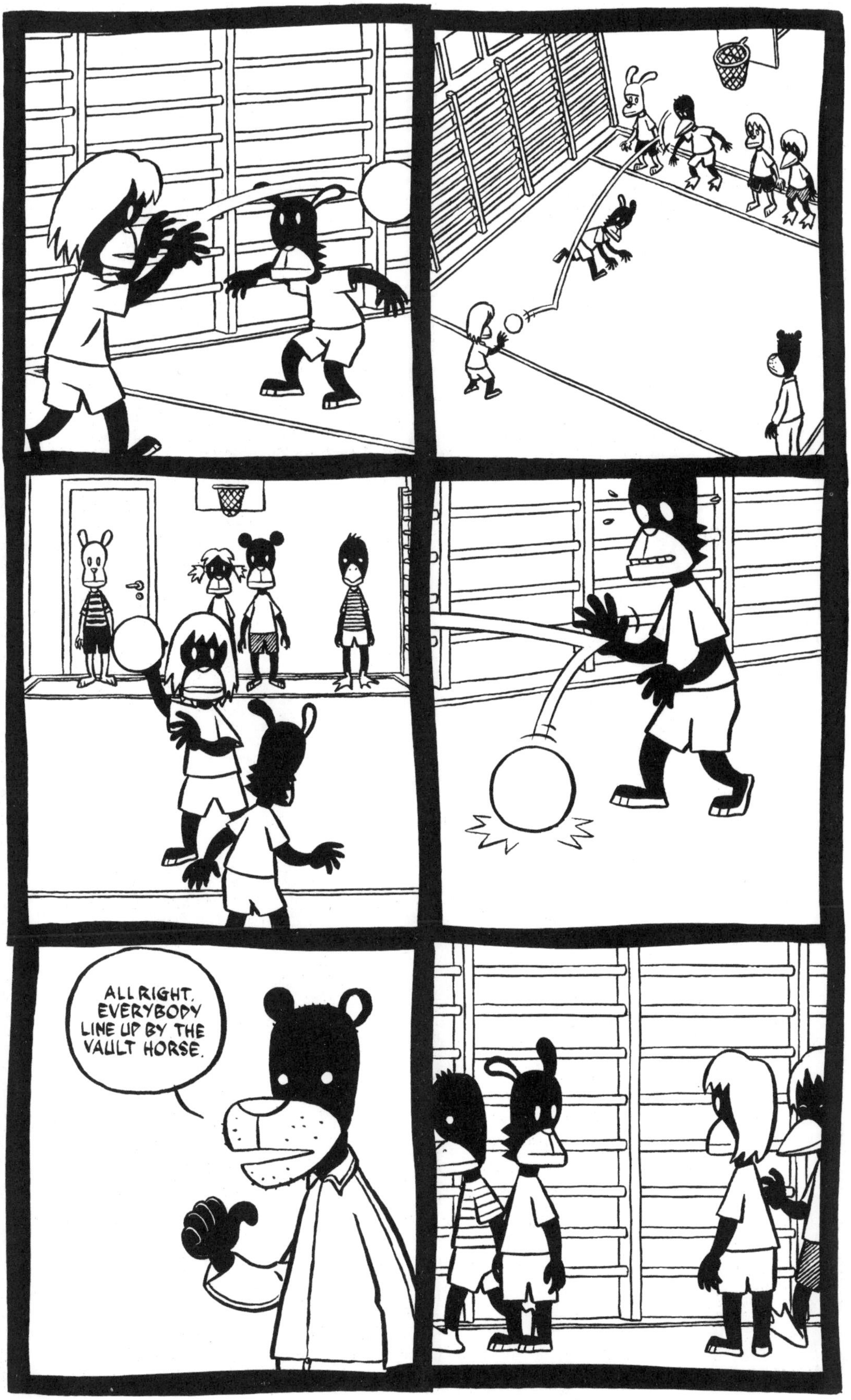
ALL RIGHT. EVERYBODY LINE UP BY THE VAULT HORSE.

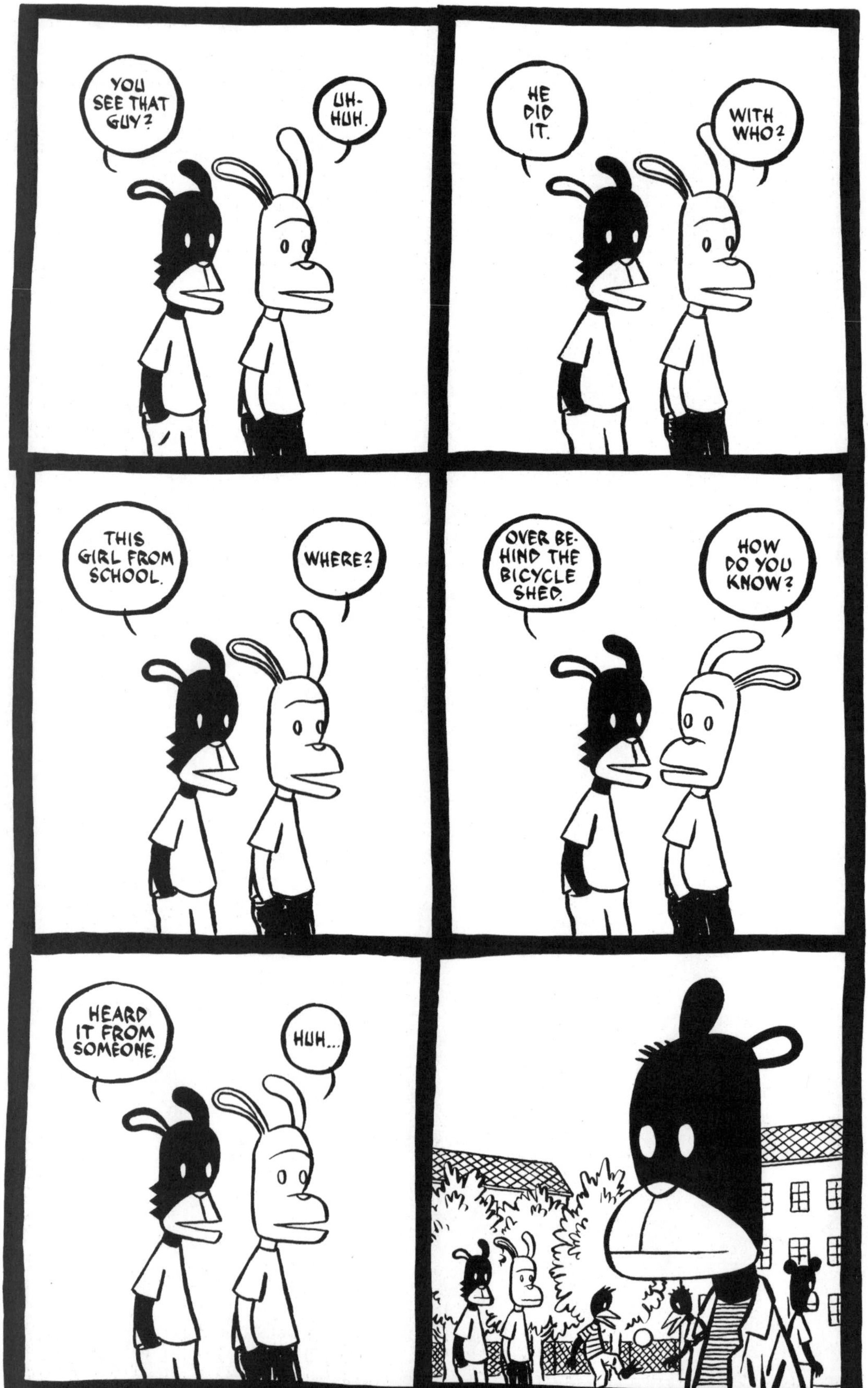
YOU SEE THAT GUY?
UH-HUH.
HE DID IT.
WITH WHO?
THIS GIRL FROM SCHOOL.
WHERE?
OVER BE-HIND THE BICYCLE SHED.
HOW DO YOU KNOW?
HEARD IT FROM SOMEONE.
HUH...

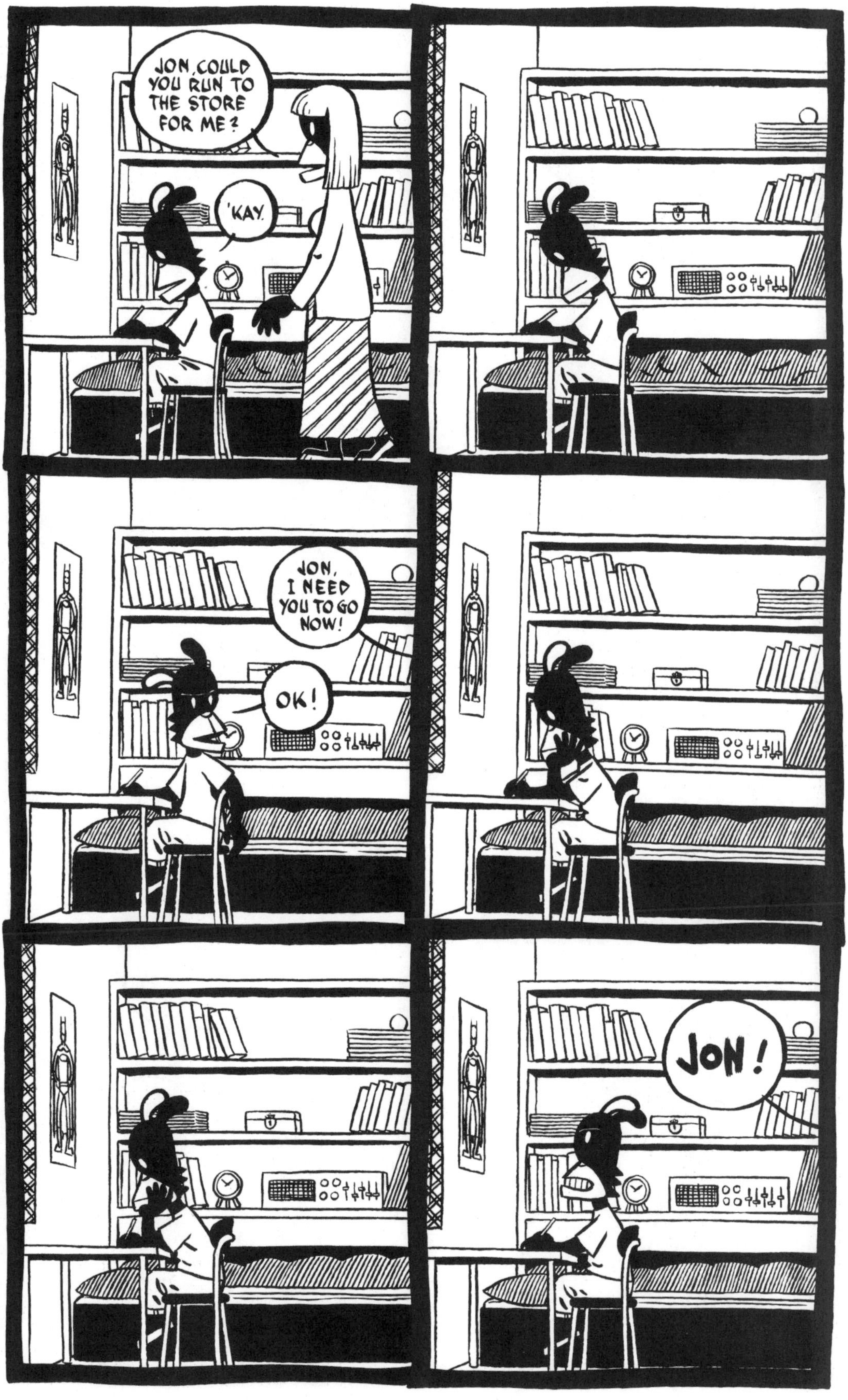
JON, COULD YOU RUN TO THE STORE FOR ME?
'KAY.
JON, I NEED YOU TO GO NOW!
OK!
JON!

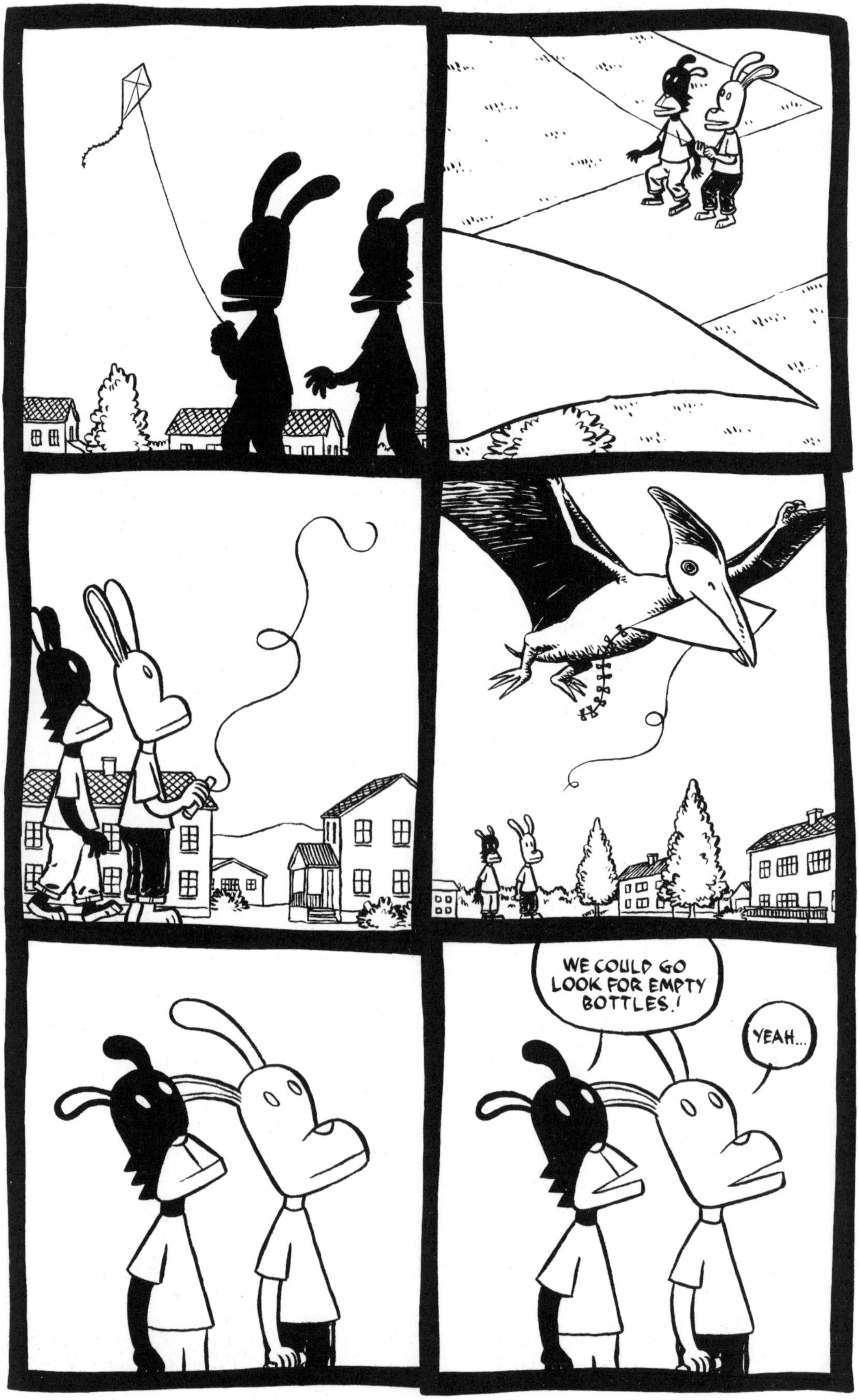
WE COULD GO LOOK FOR EMPTY BOTTLES.!
YEAH...

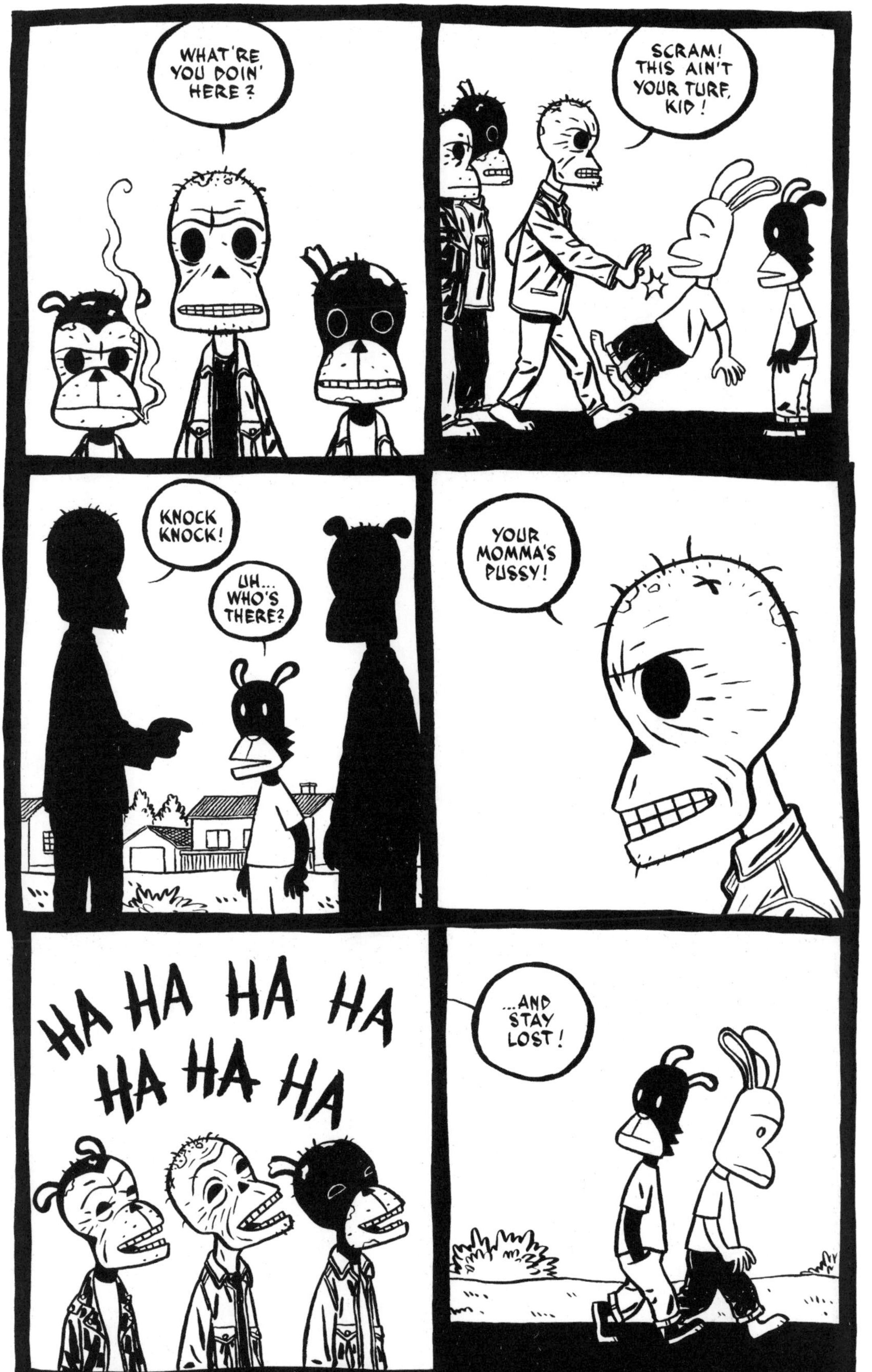
WHAT'RE YOU DOIN' HERE?
SCRAM! THIS AIN'T YOUR TURF, KID!
KNOCK KNOCK!
UH... WHO'S THERE?
YOUR MOMMA'S PUSSY!
HA HA HA HA
HA HA HA
...AND STAY LOST!

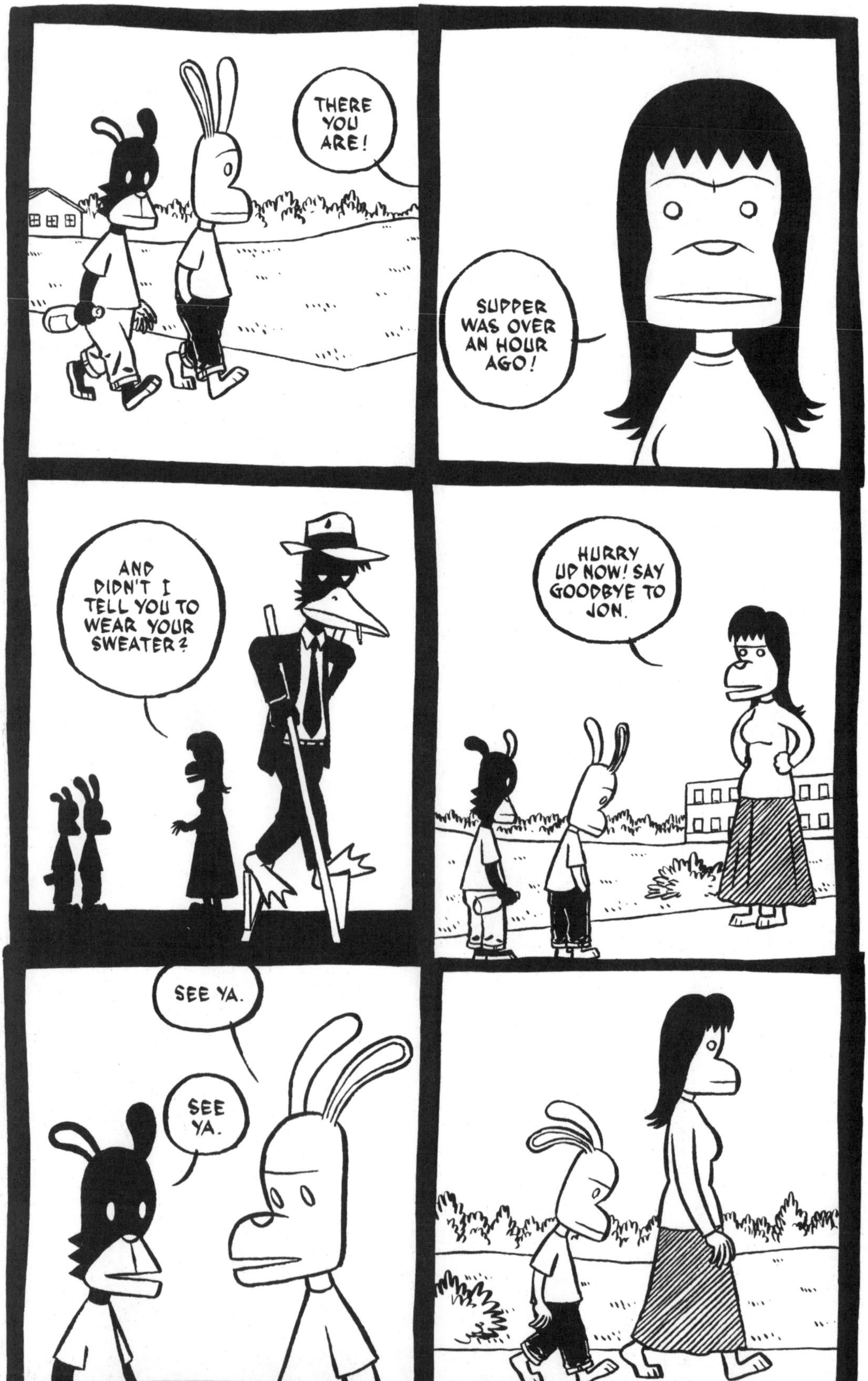
THERE YOU ARE!
SUPPER WAS OVER AN HOUR AGO!
AND DIDN'T I TELL YOU TO WEAR YOUR SWEATER?
HURRY UP NOW! SAY GOODBYE TO JON.
SEE YA.
SEE YA.

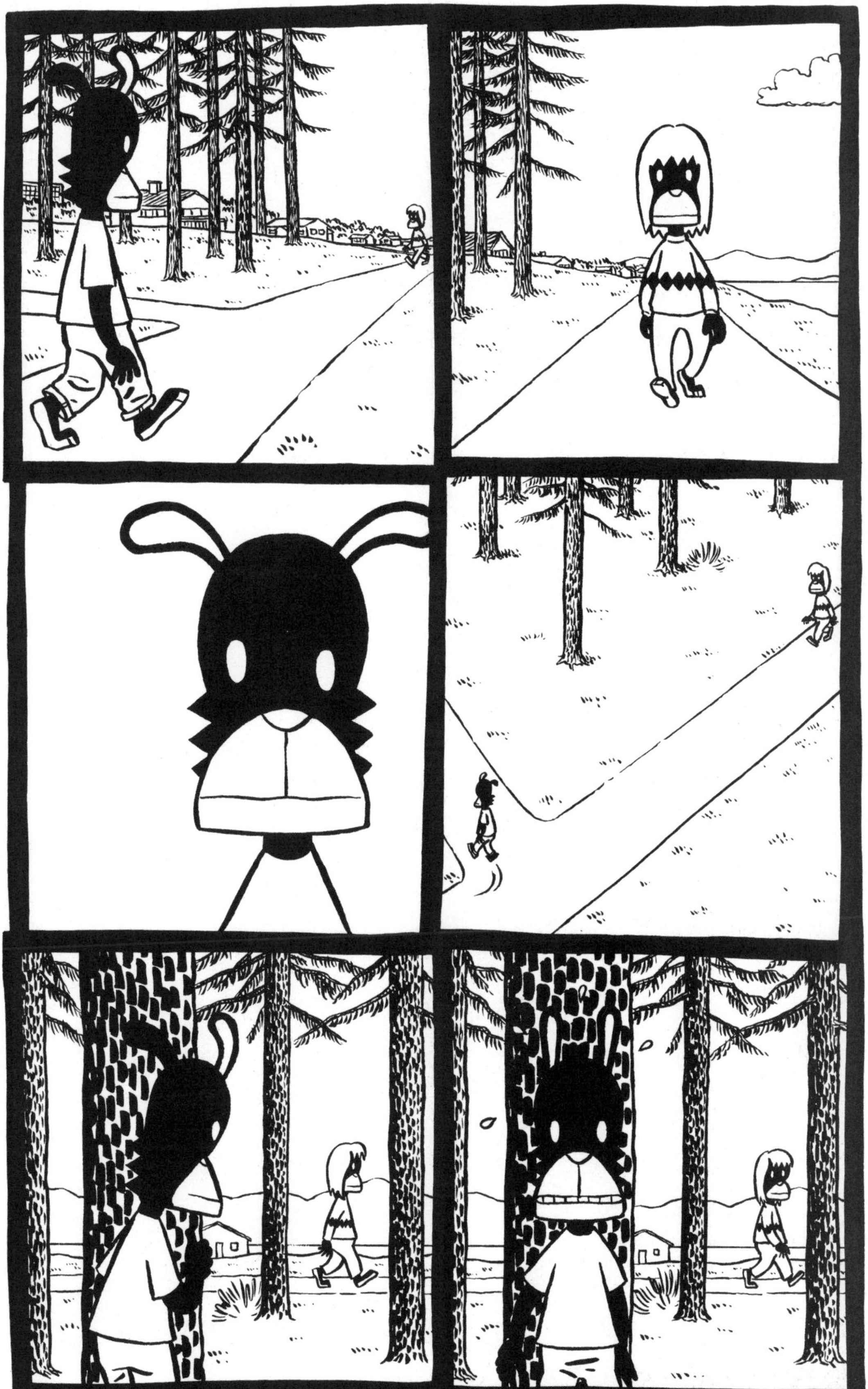

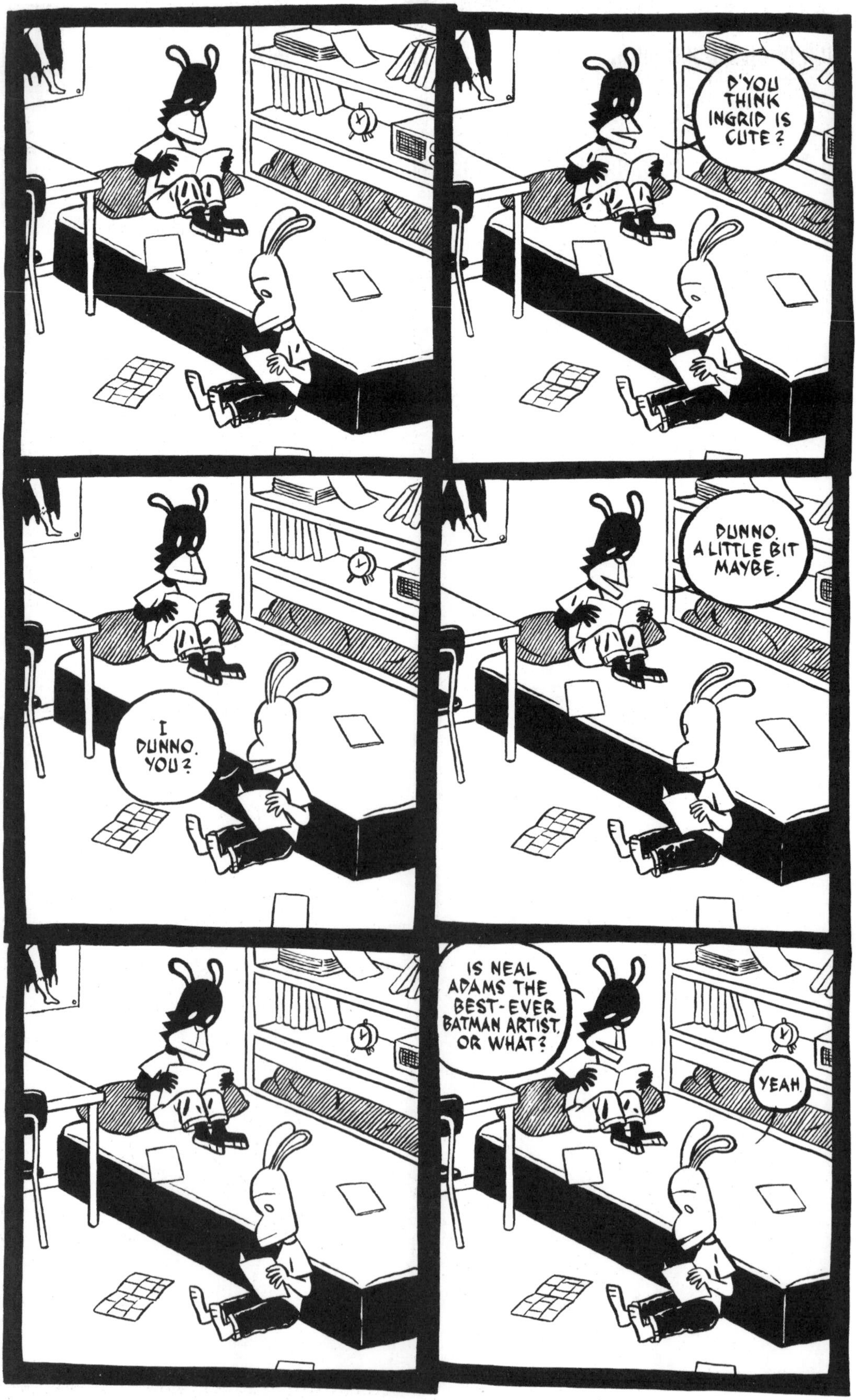
D'YOU THINK INGRID IS CUTE?
I DUNNO. YOU?
DUNNO. A LITTLE BIT MAYBE.
IS NEAL ADAMS THE BEST-EVER BATMAN ARTIST, OR WHAT?
YEAH.

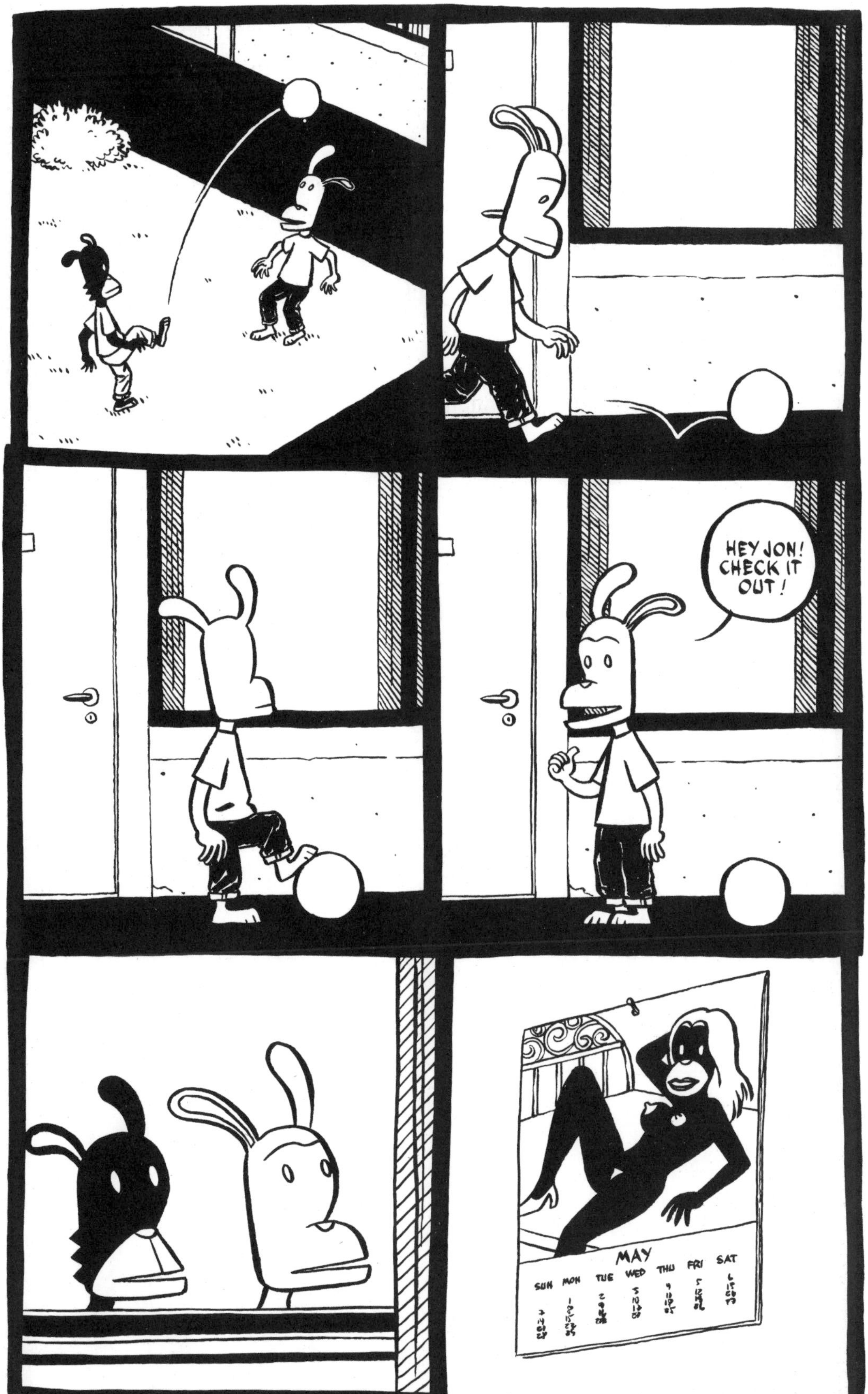
HEY JON! CHECK IT OUT!
MAY
SUN MON TUE WED THU FRI SAT

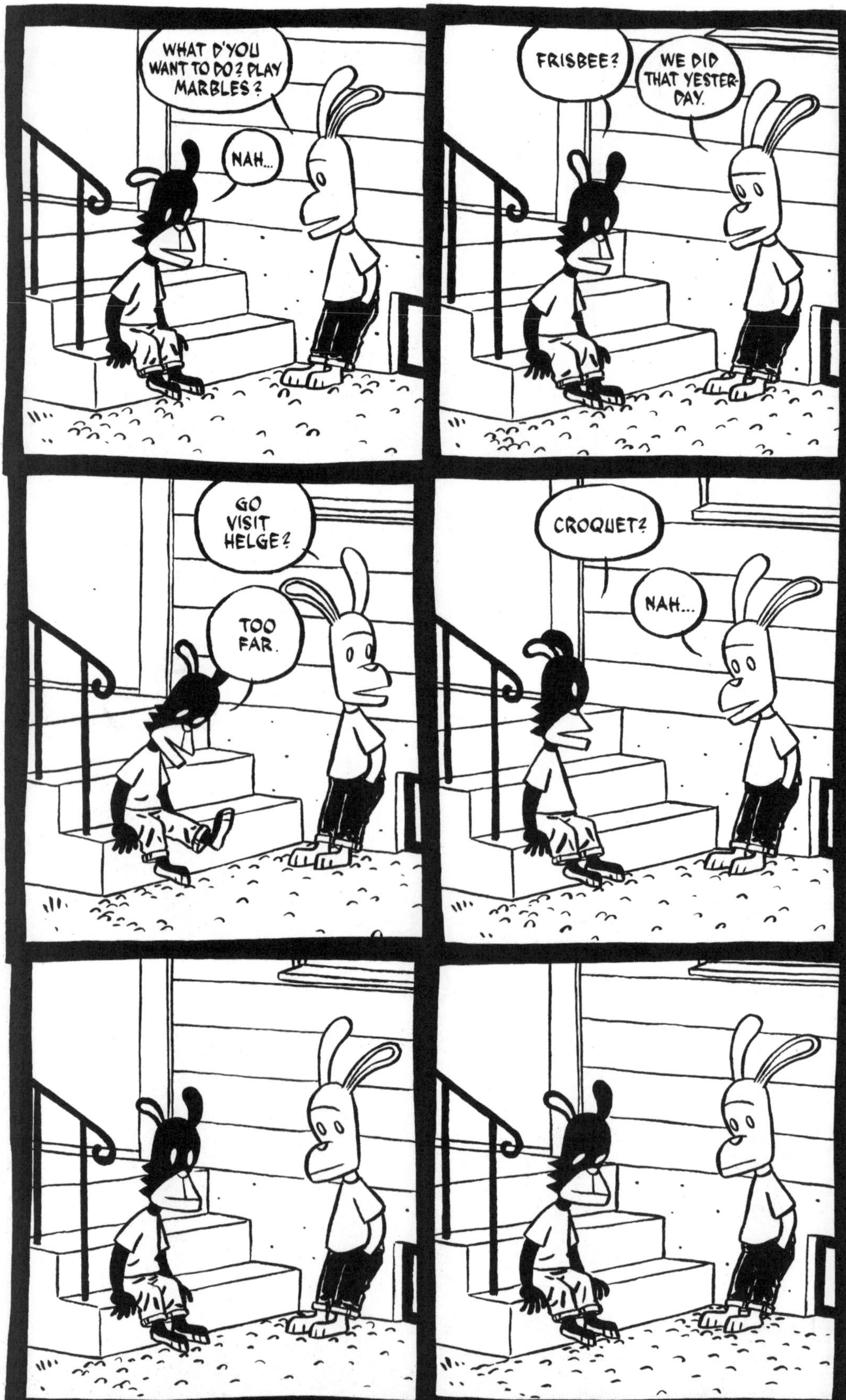
WHAT D'YOU WANT TO DO? PLAY MARBLES?
NAH...
FRISBEE?
WE DID THAT YESTER-DAY.
GO VISIT HELGE?
TOO FAR.
CROQUET?
NAH...

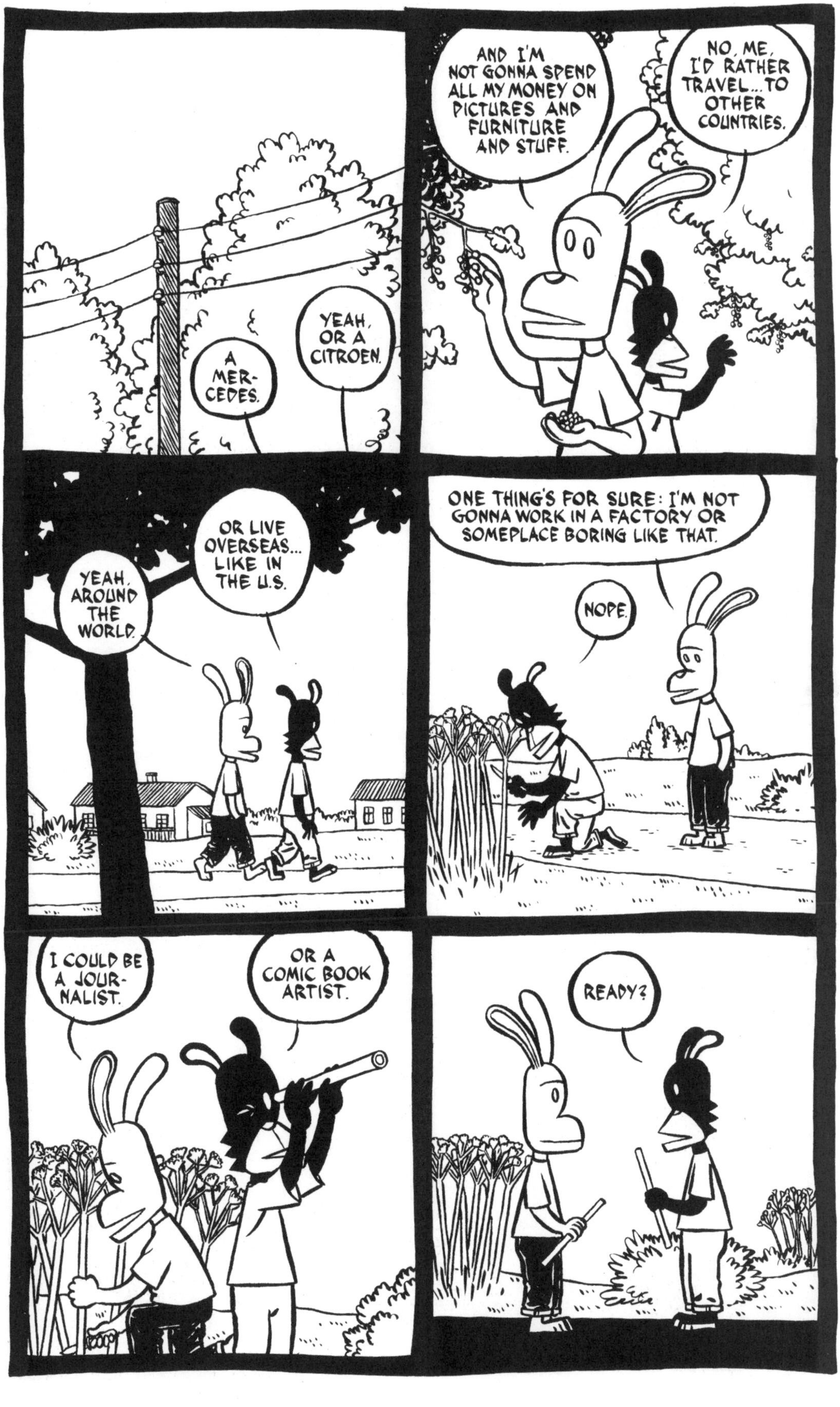
A MER-CEDES.
YEAH, OR A CITROEN.
AND I'M NOT GONNA SPEND ALL MY MONEY ON PICTURES AND FURNITURE AND STUFF.
NO, ME, I'D RATHER TRAVEL... TO OTHER COUNTRIES.
YEAH, AROUND THE WORLD.
OR LIVE OVERSEAS... LIKE IN THE U.S.
ONE THING'S FOR SURE: I'M NOT GONNA WORK IN A FACTORY OR SOMEPLACE BORING LIKE THAT.
NOPE.
I COULD BE A JOUR-NALIST.
OR A COMIC BOOK ARTIST.
READY?

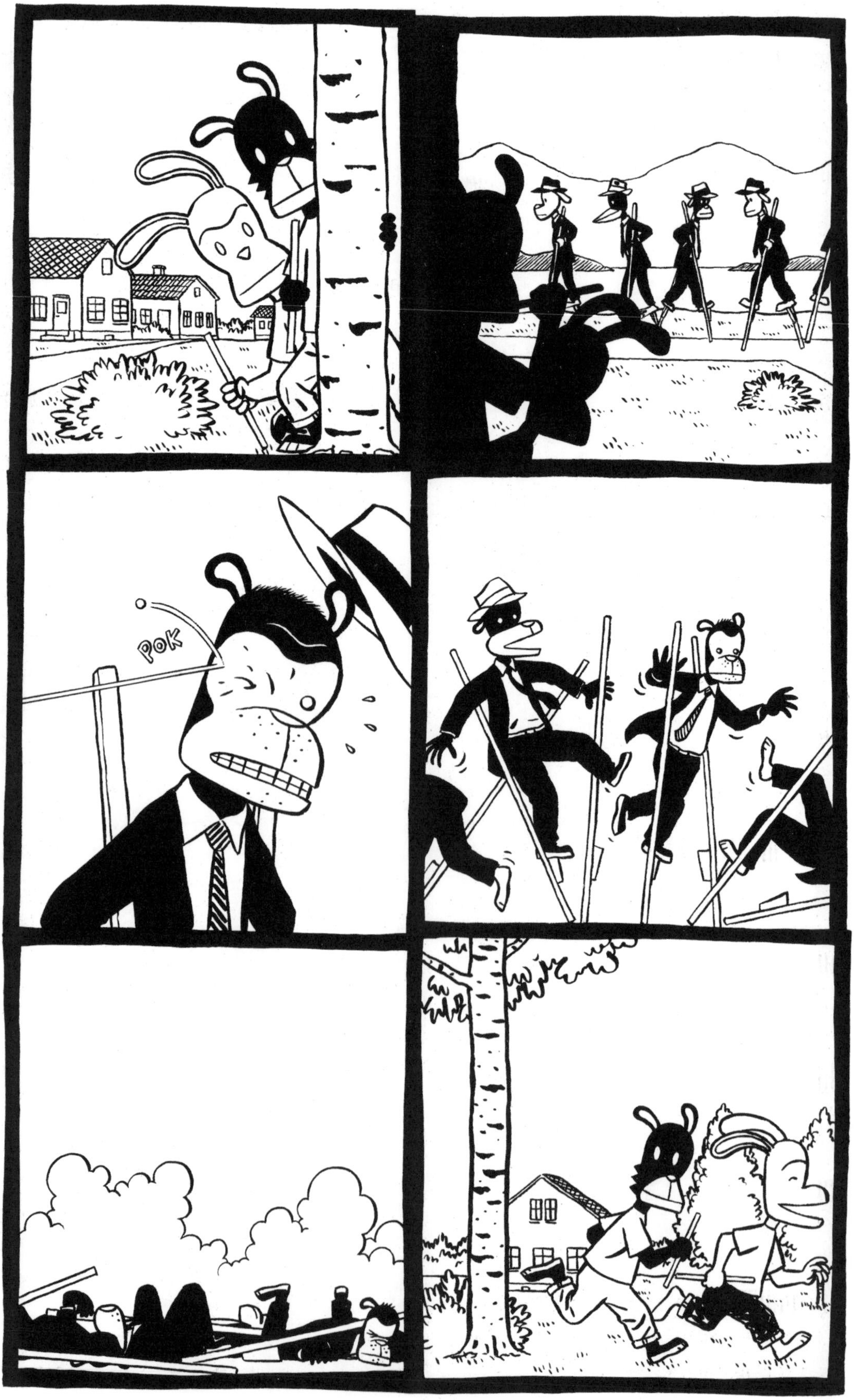
POK

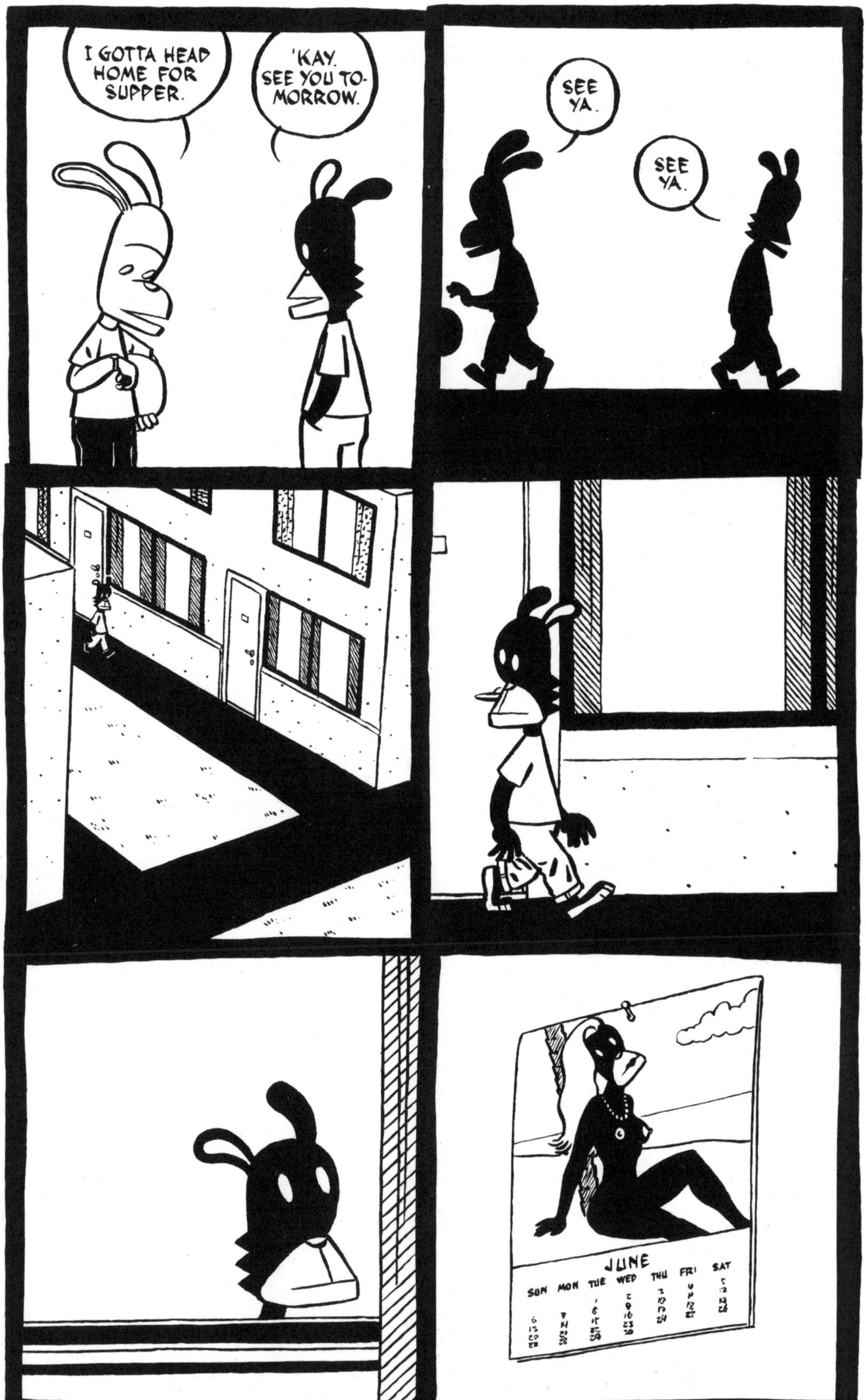
I GOTTA HEAD HOME FOR SUPPER.
'KAY. SEE YOU TO-MORROW.
SEE YA.
SEE YA.
JUNE
SUN MON TUE WED THU FRI SAT

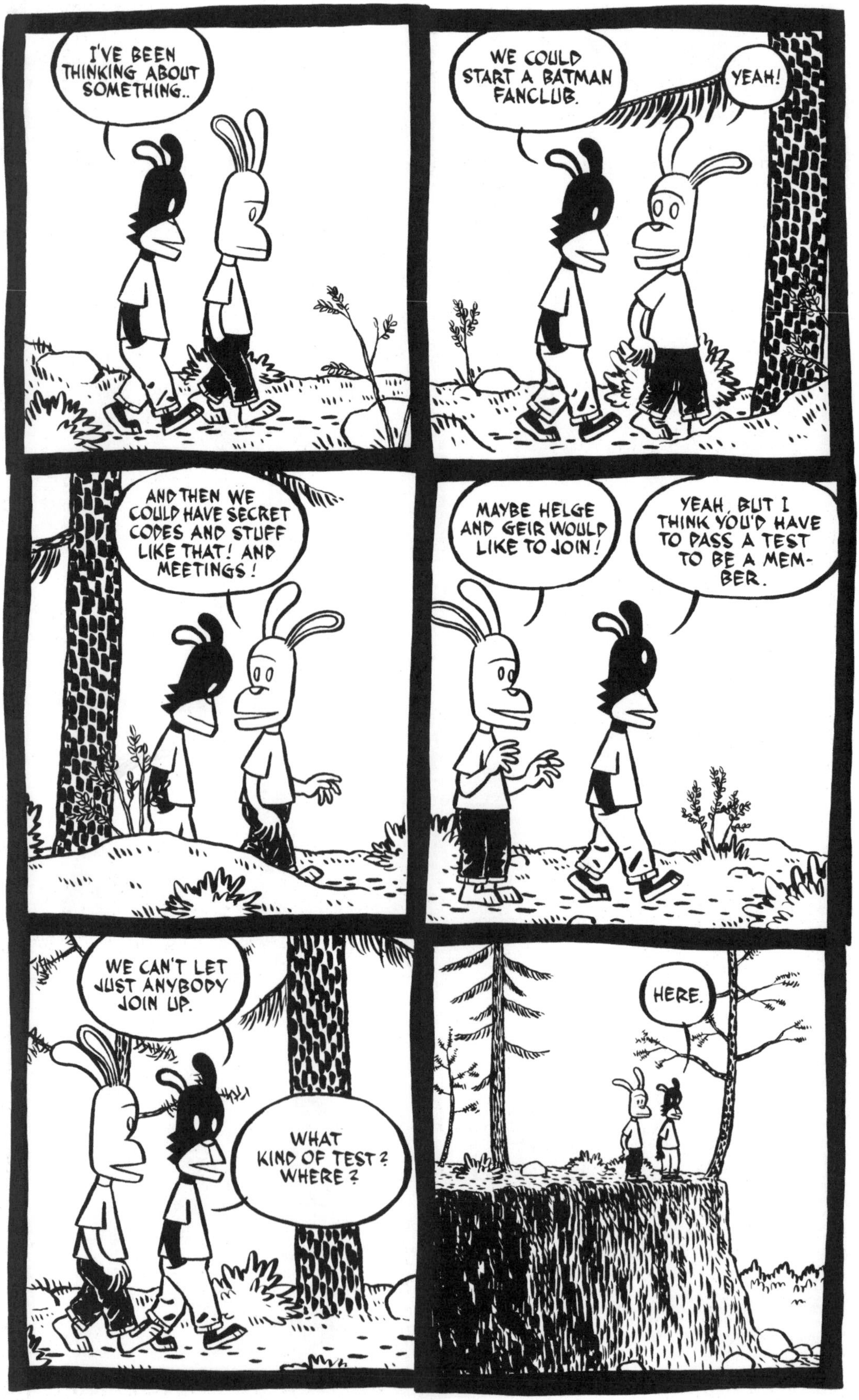

I'VE BEEN THINKING ABOUT SOMETHING..
WE COULD START A BATMAN FANCLUB.
YEAH!
AND THEN WE COULD HAVE SECRET CODES AND STUFF LIKE THAT! AND MEETINGS!
MAYBE HELGE AND GEIR WOULD LIKE TO JOIN!
YEAH, BUT I THINK YOU'D HAVE TO PASS A TEST TO BE A MEM-BER.
WE CAN'T LET JUST ANYBODY JOIN UP.
WHAT KIND OF TEST? WHERE?
HERE.

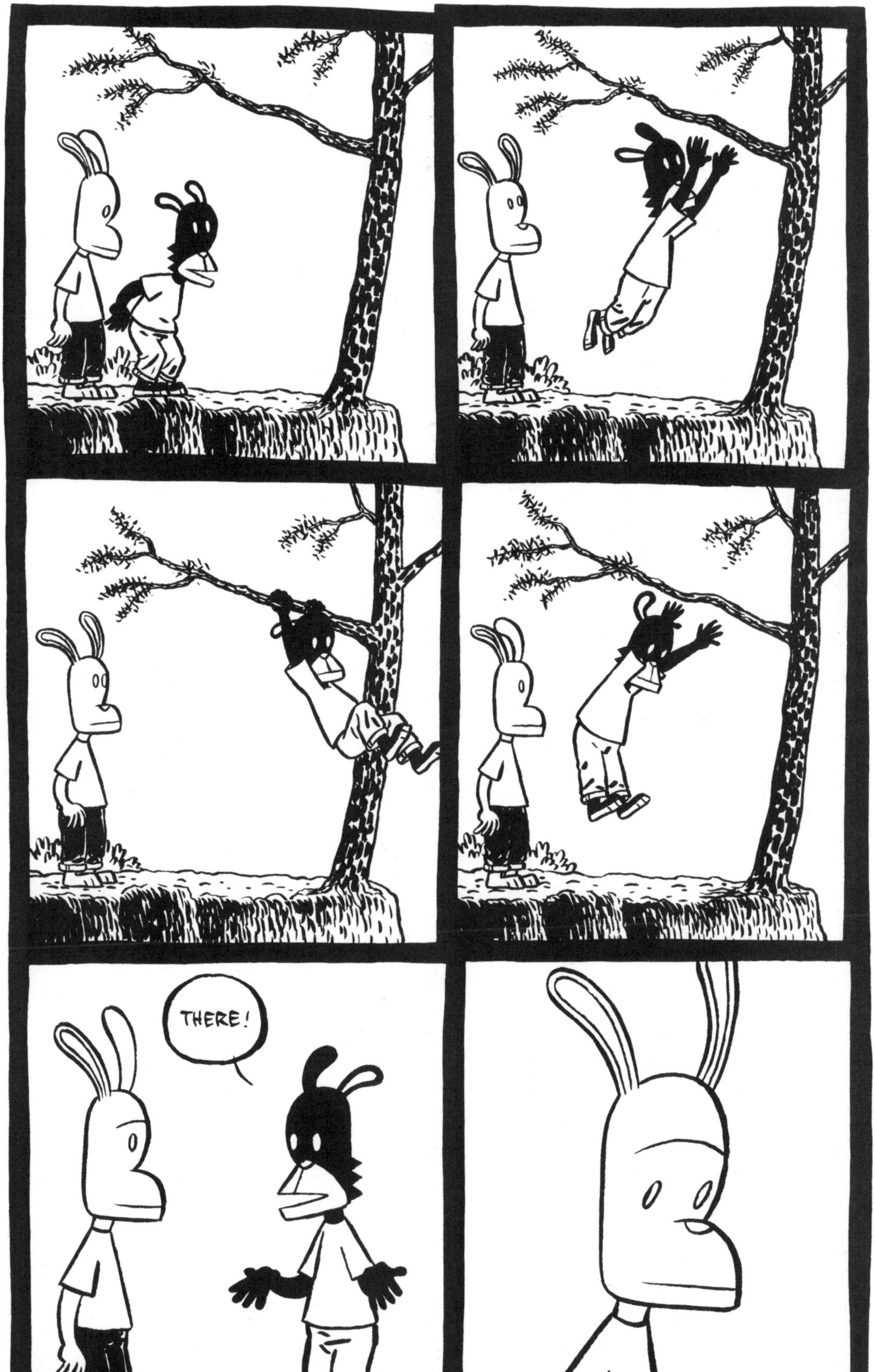
THERE!

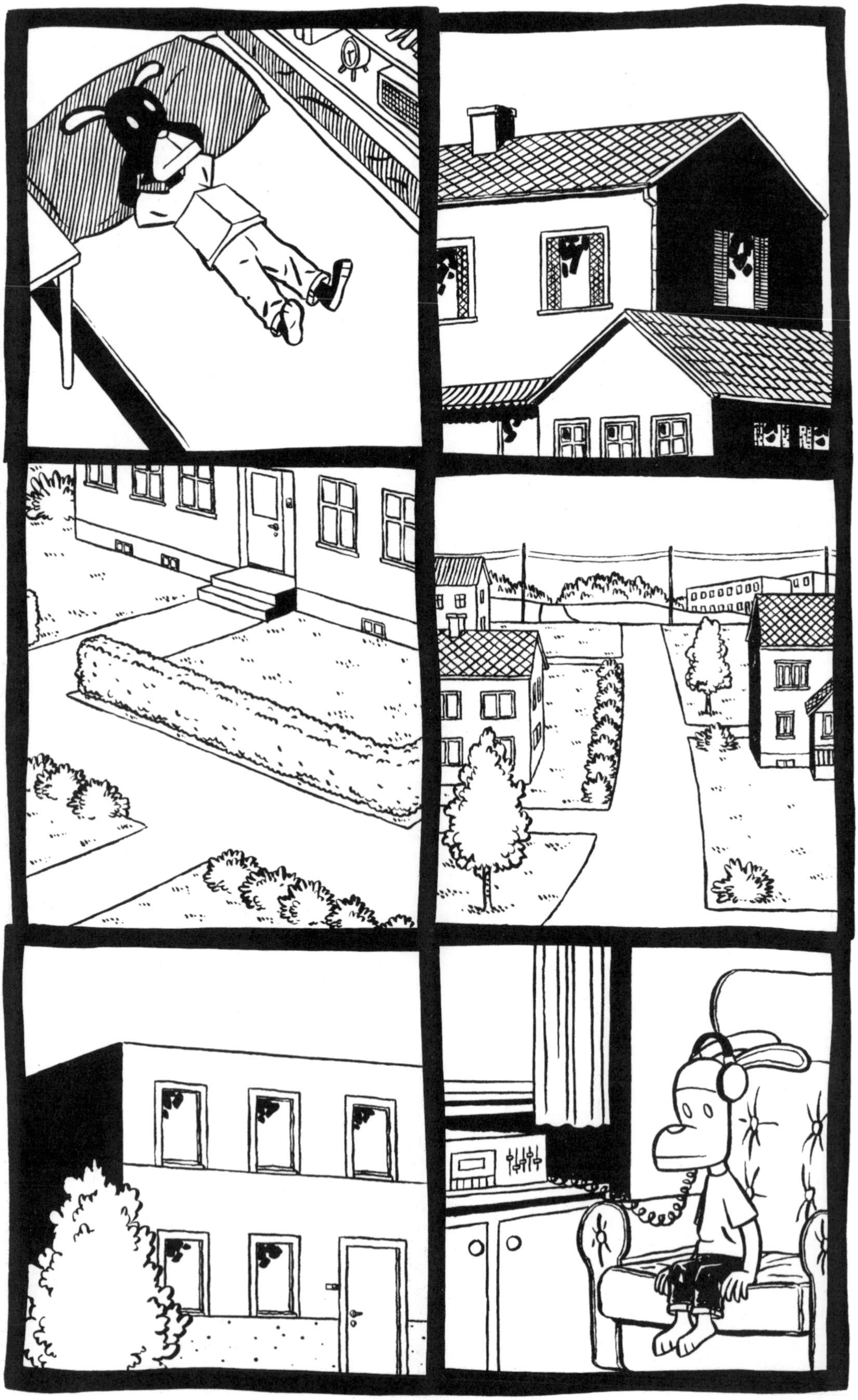

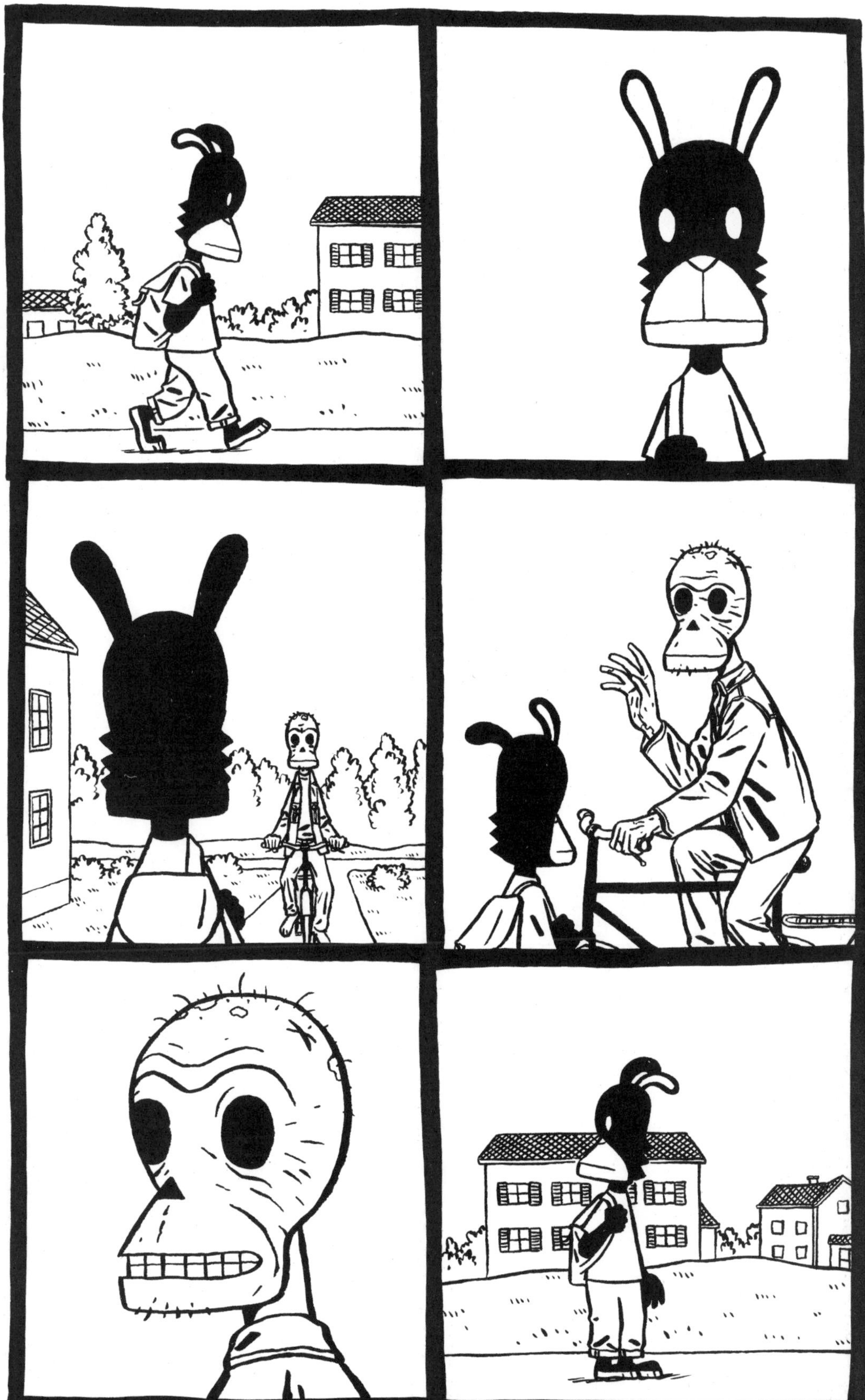

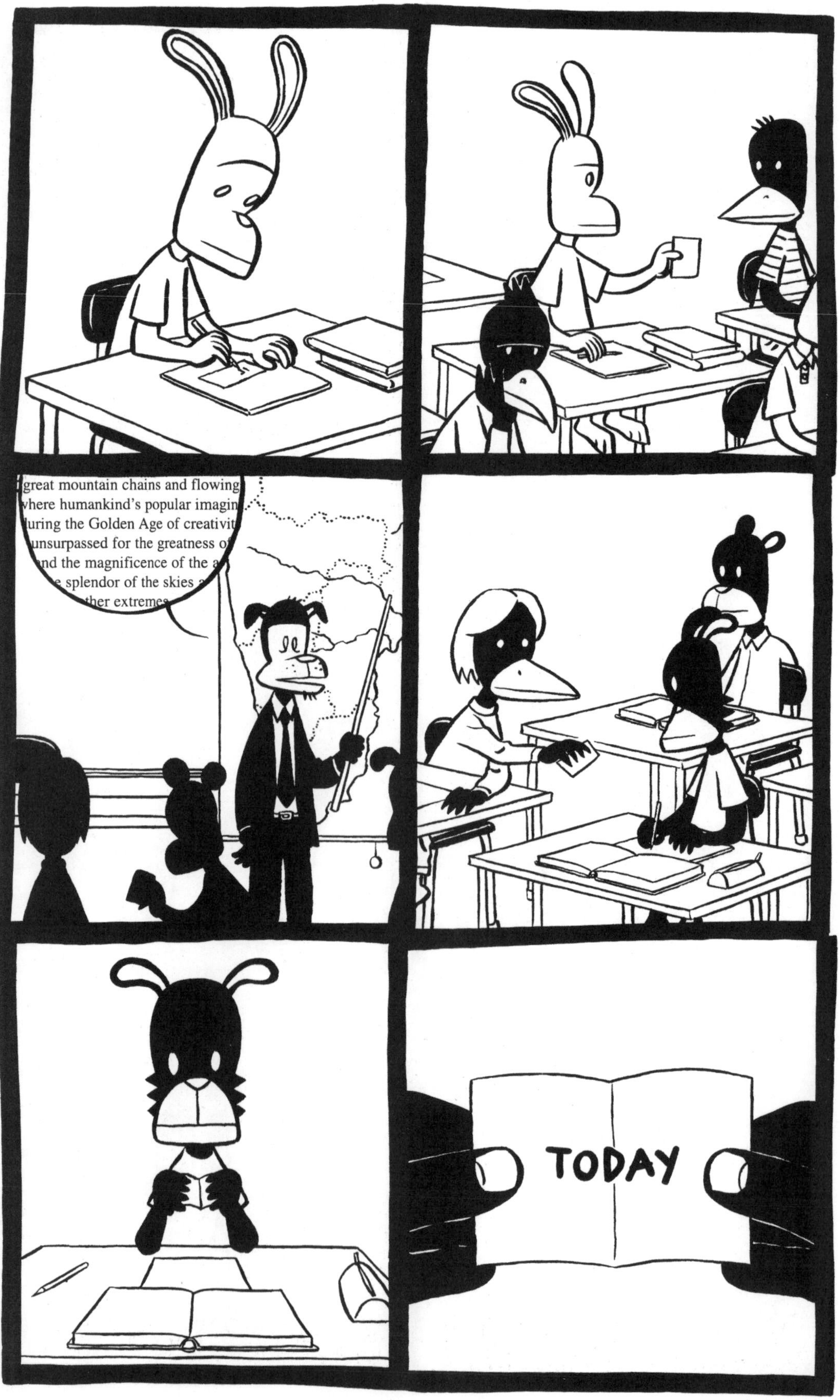
great mountain chains and flowing
where humankind's popular imagin
during the Golden Age of creativit
unsurpassed for the greatness o
and the magnificence of the a
splendor of the skies a
ther extremes
TODAY

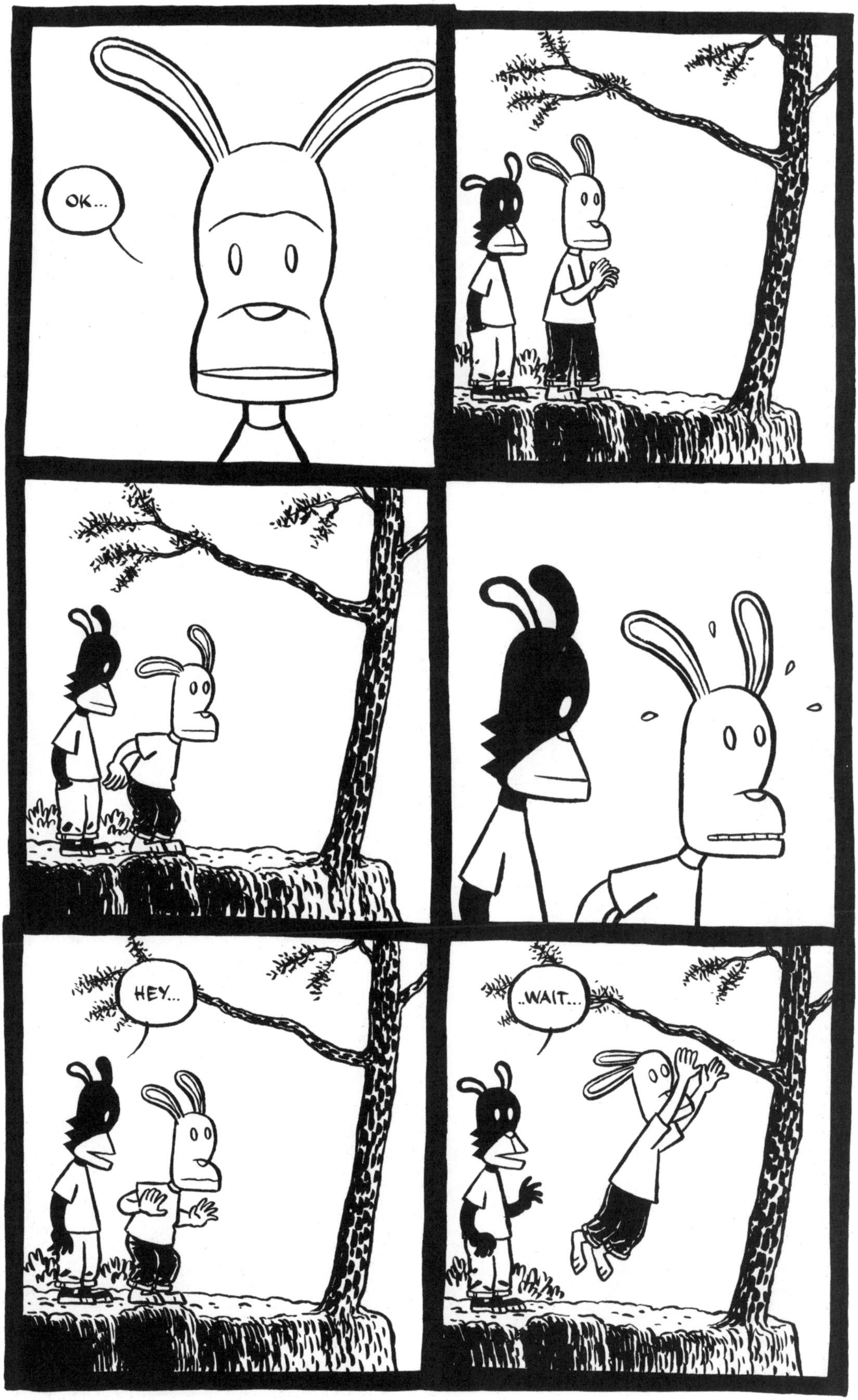
OK...
HEY...
..WAIT...

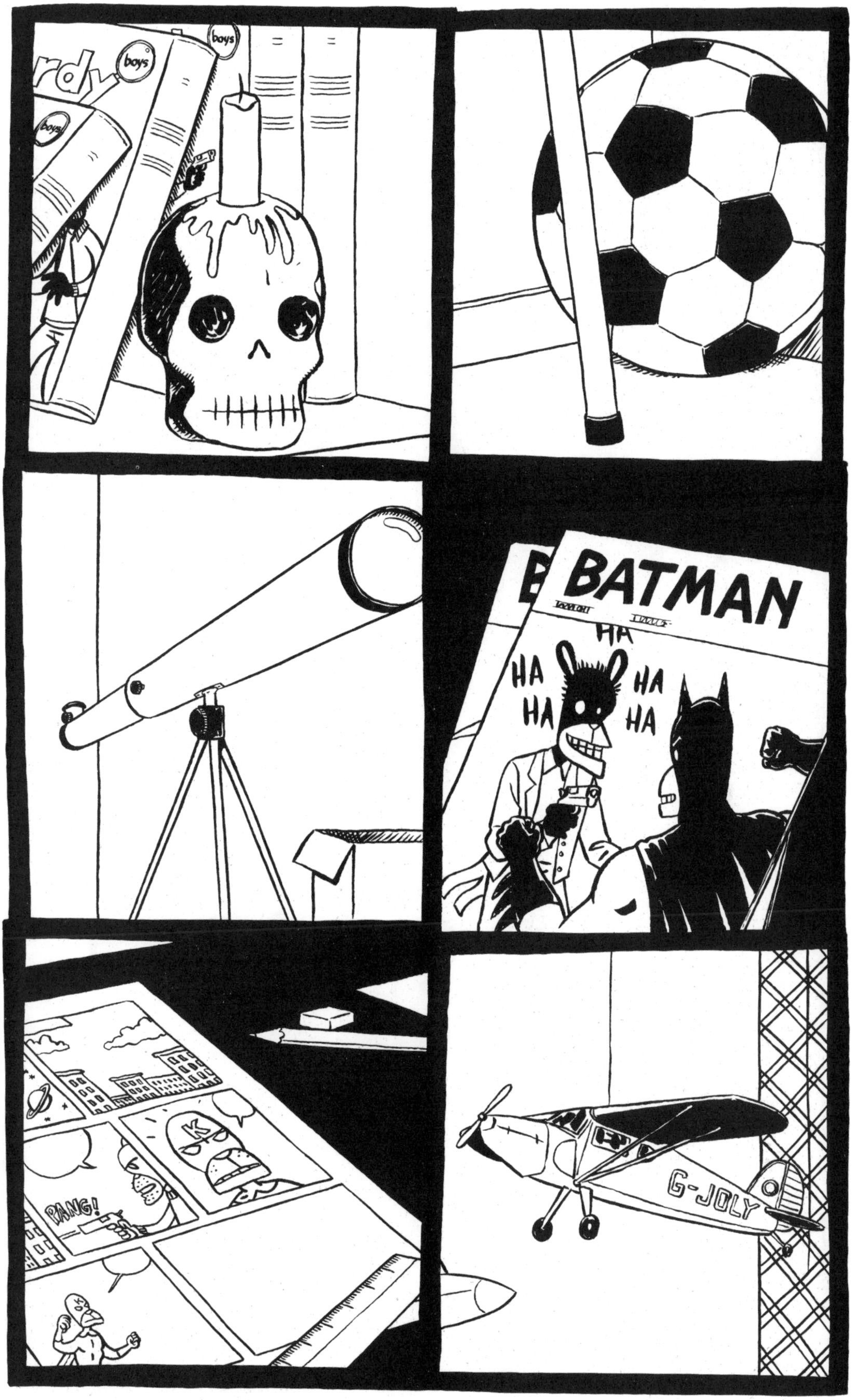

rdy
boys
boys
boys
boys
BATMAN
HA
HA
HA
HA
HA
HA
PANG!
K
G-JOLY

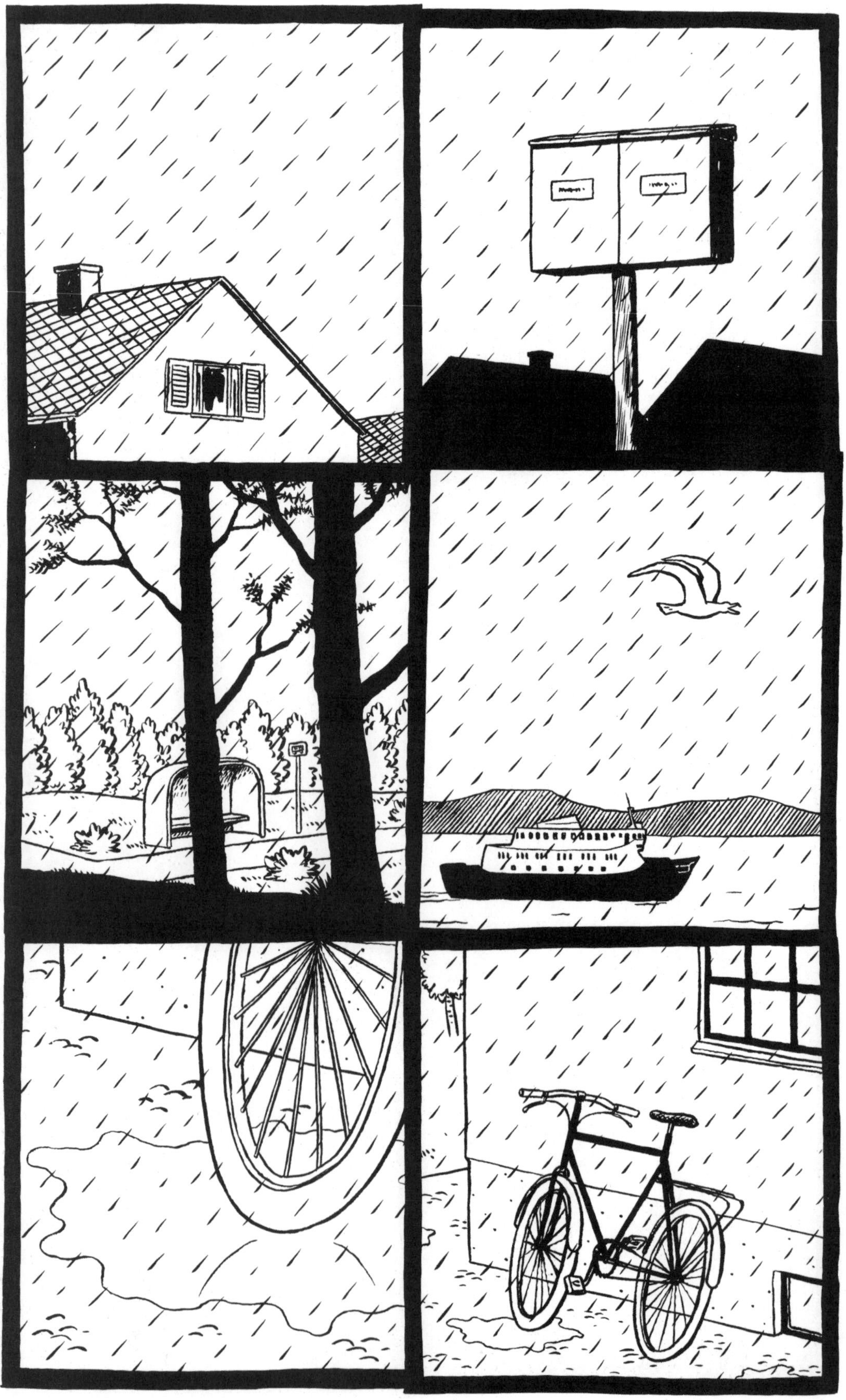

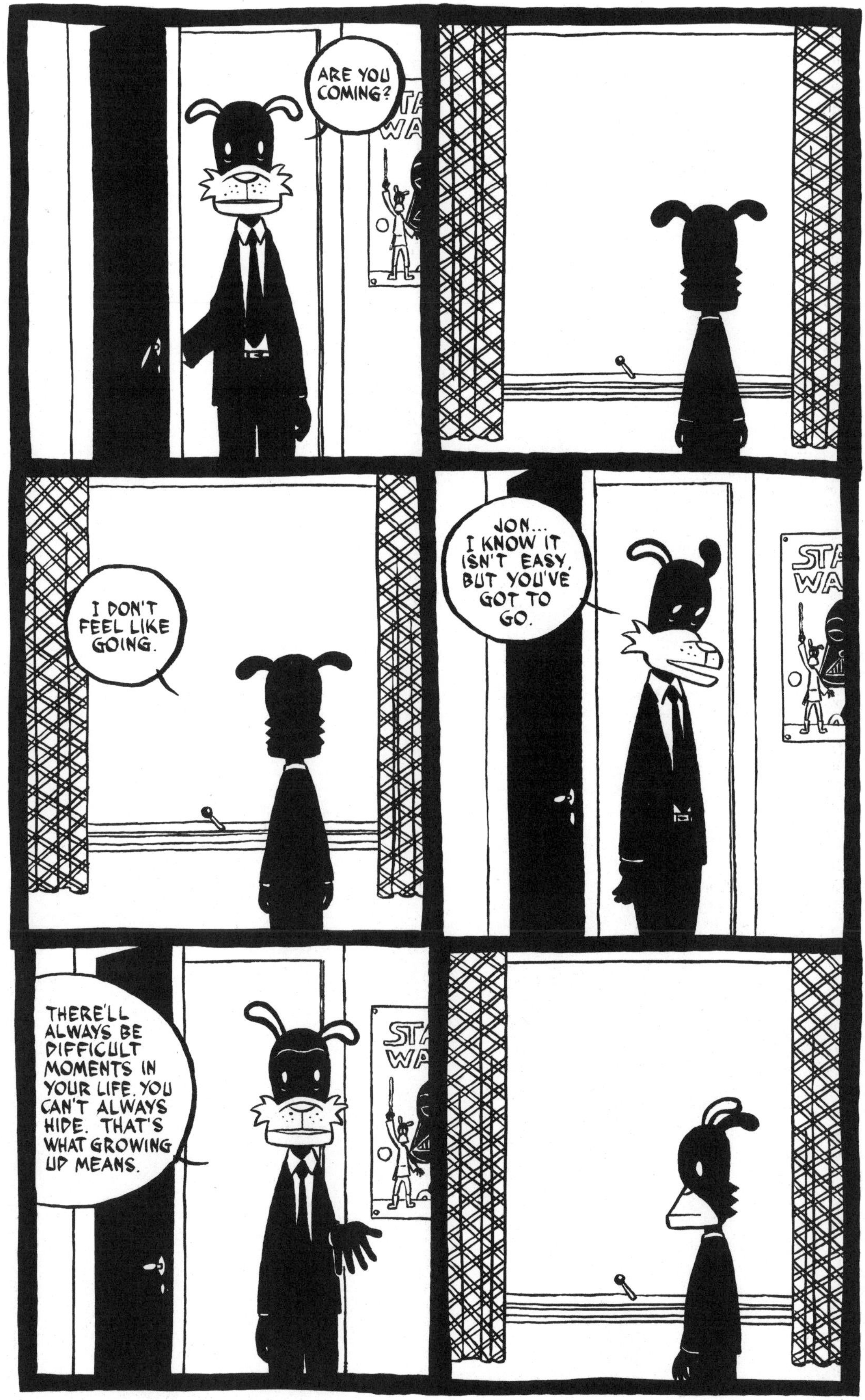

ARE YOU COMING?
STA WA
I DON'T FEEL LIKE GOING.
JON... I KNOW IT ISN'T EASY, BUT YOU'VE GOT TO GO.
STA WA
THERE'LL ALWAYS BE DIFFICULT MOMENTS IN YOUR LIFE. YOU CAN'T ALWAYS HIDE. THAT'S WHAT GROWING UP MEANS.
STA WA

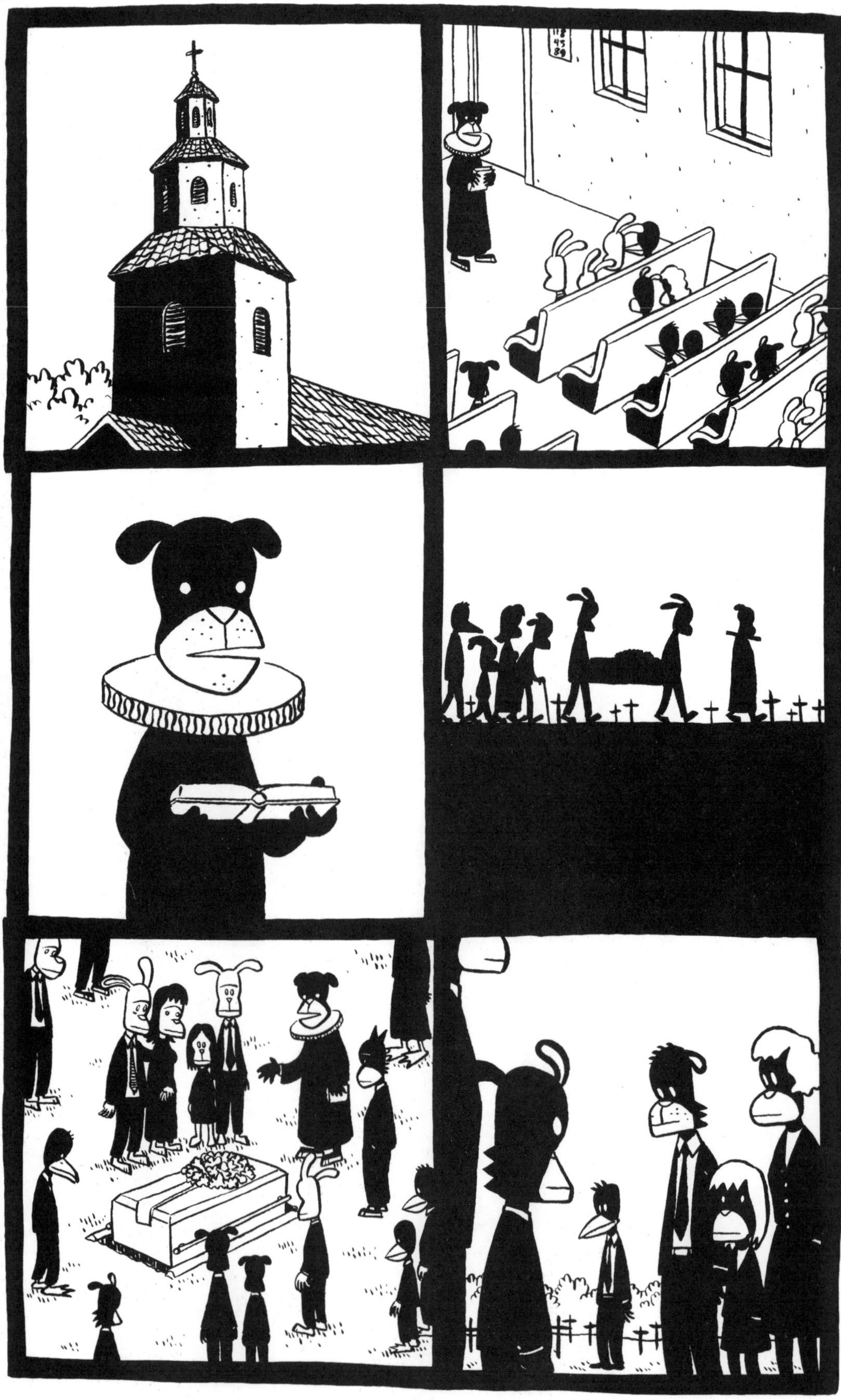
118
45
89

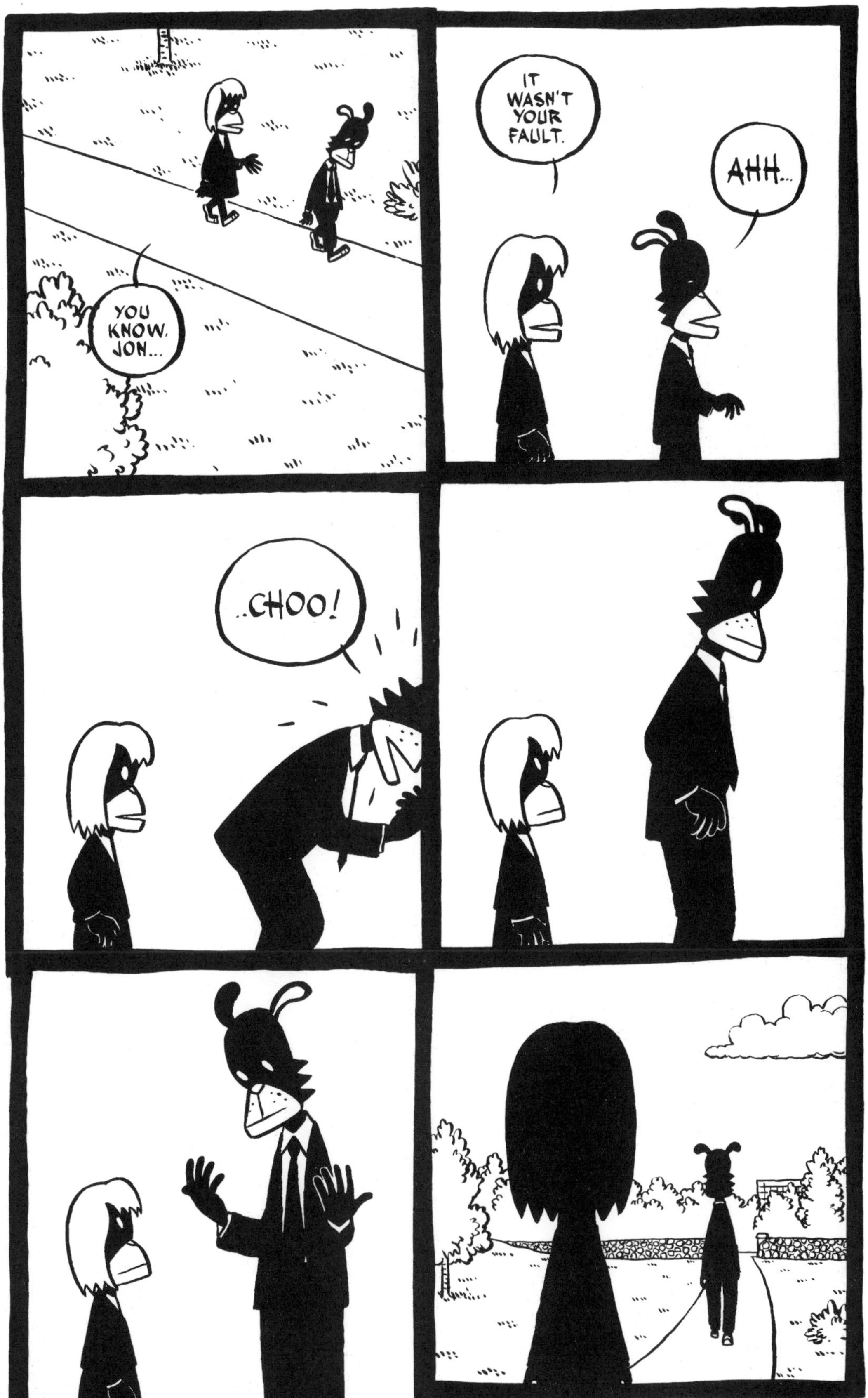
YOU KNOW, JON...
IT WASN'T YOUR FAULT.
AHH...
..CHOO!

END OF PART ONE

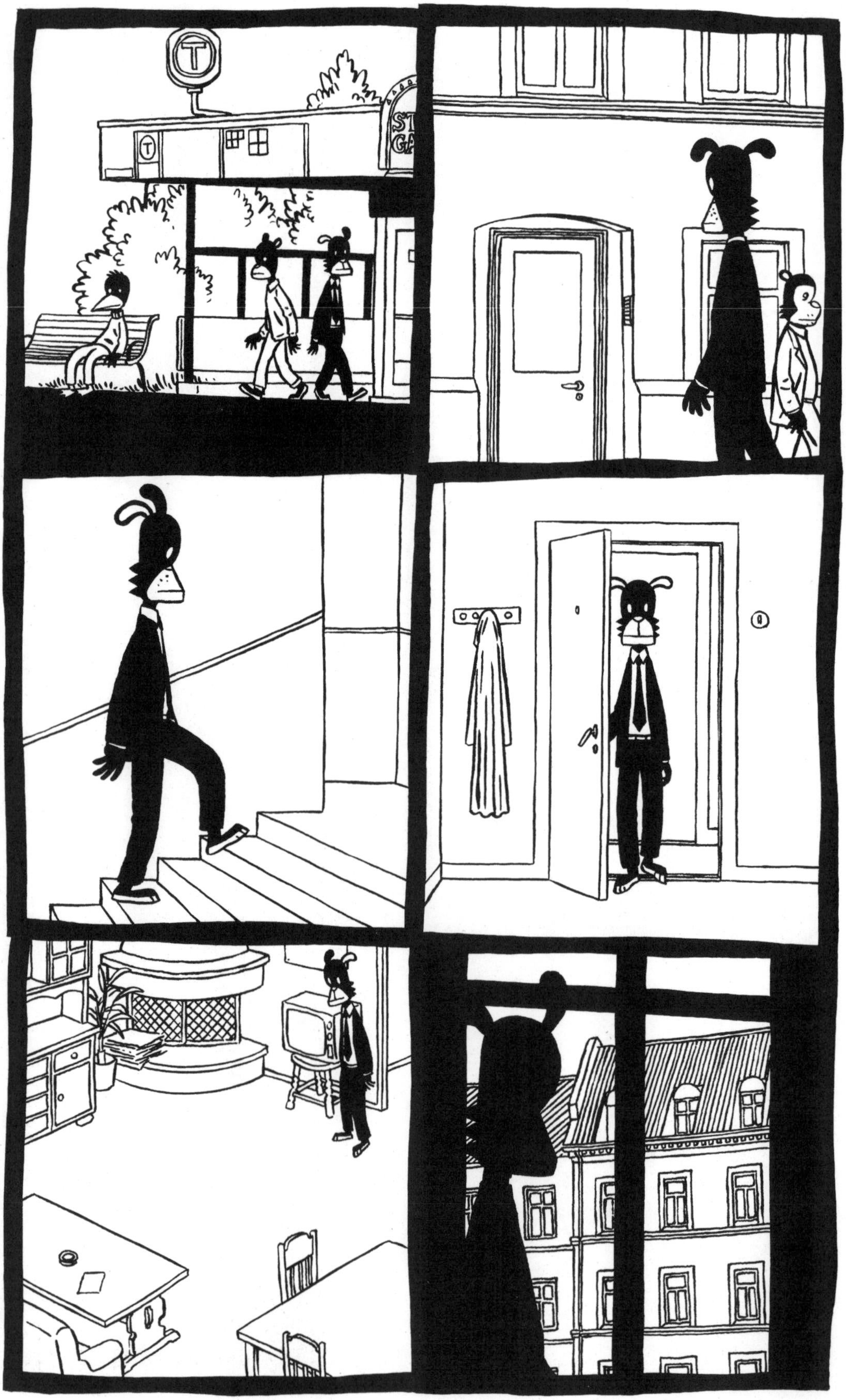

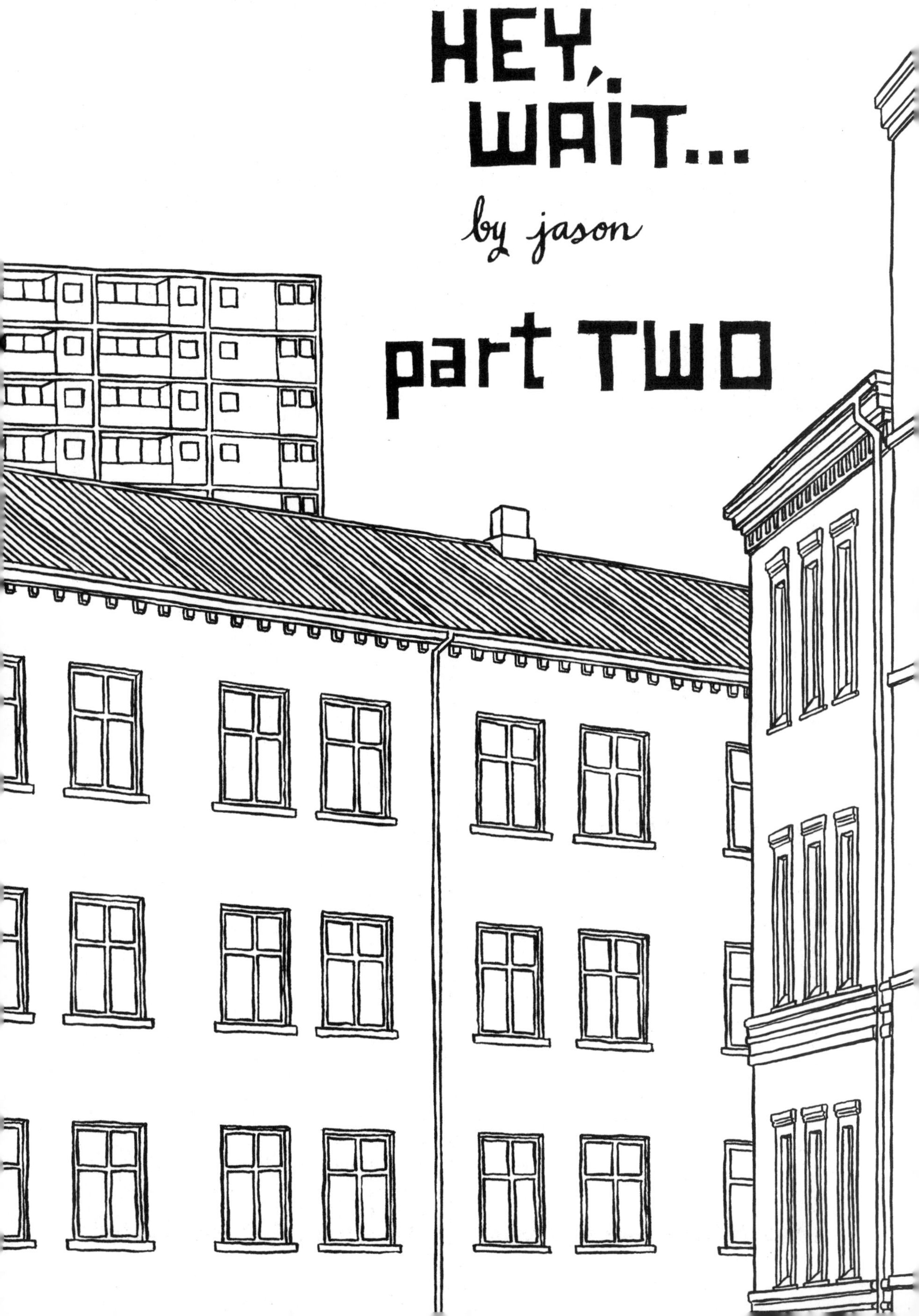
HEY, WAIT...
by jason
part TWO

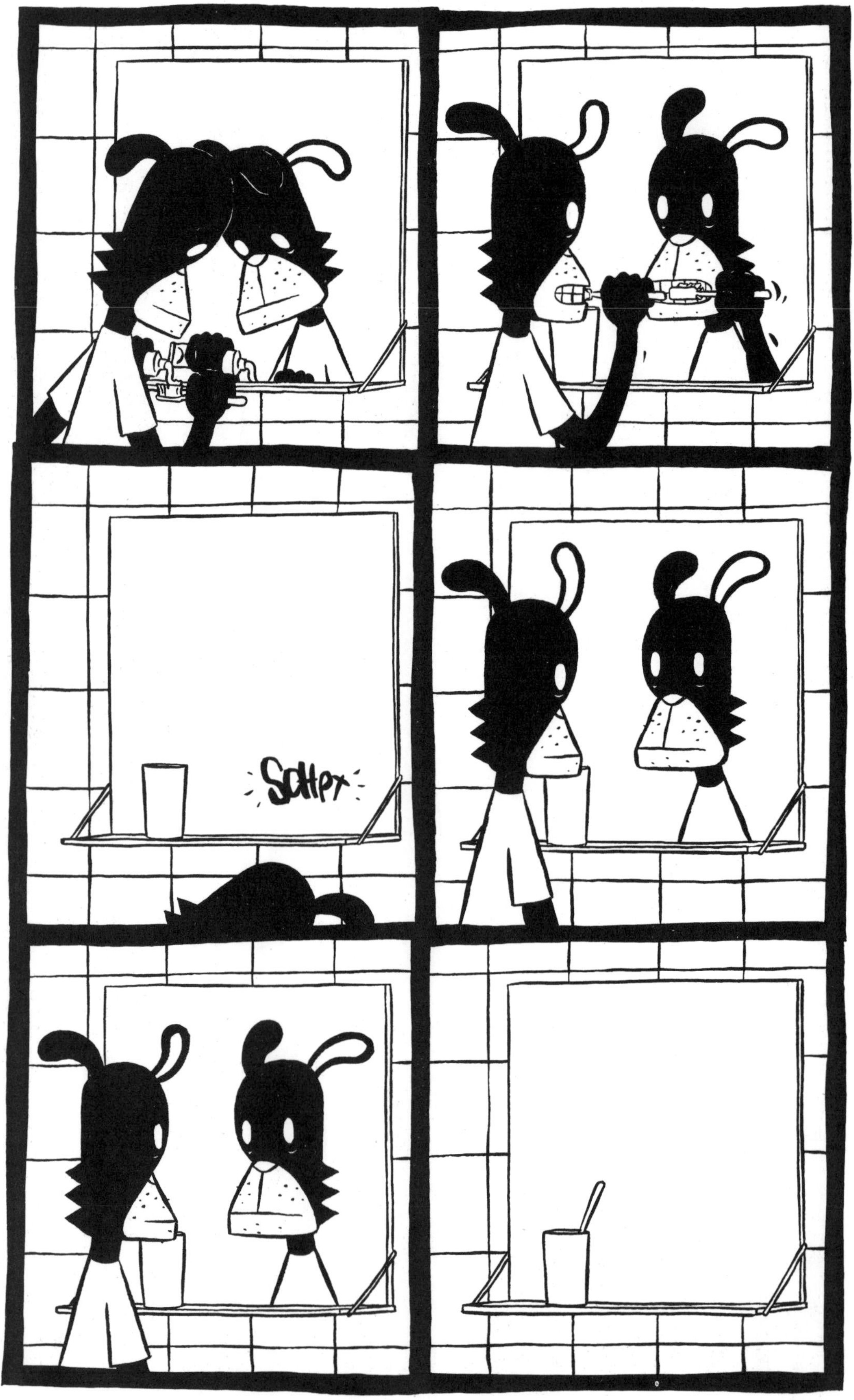
SCHPT

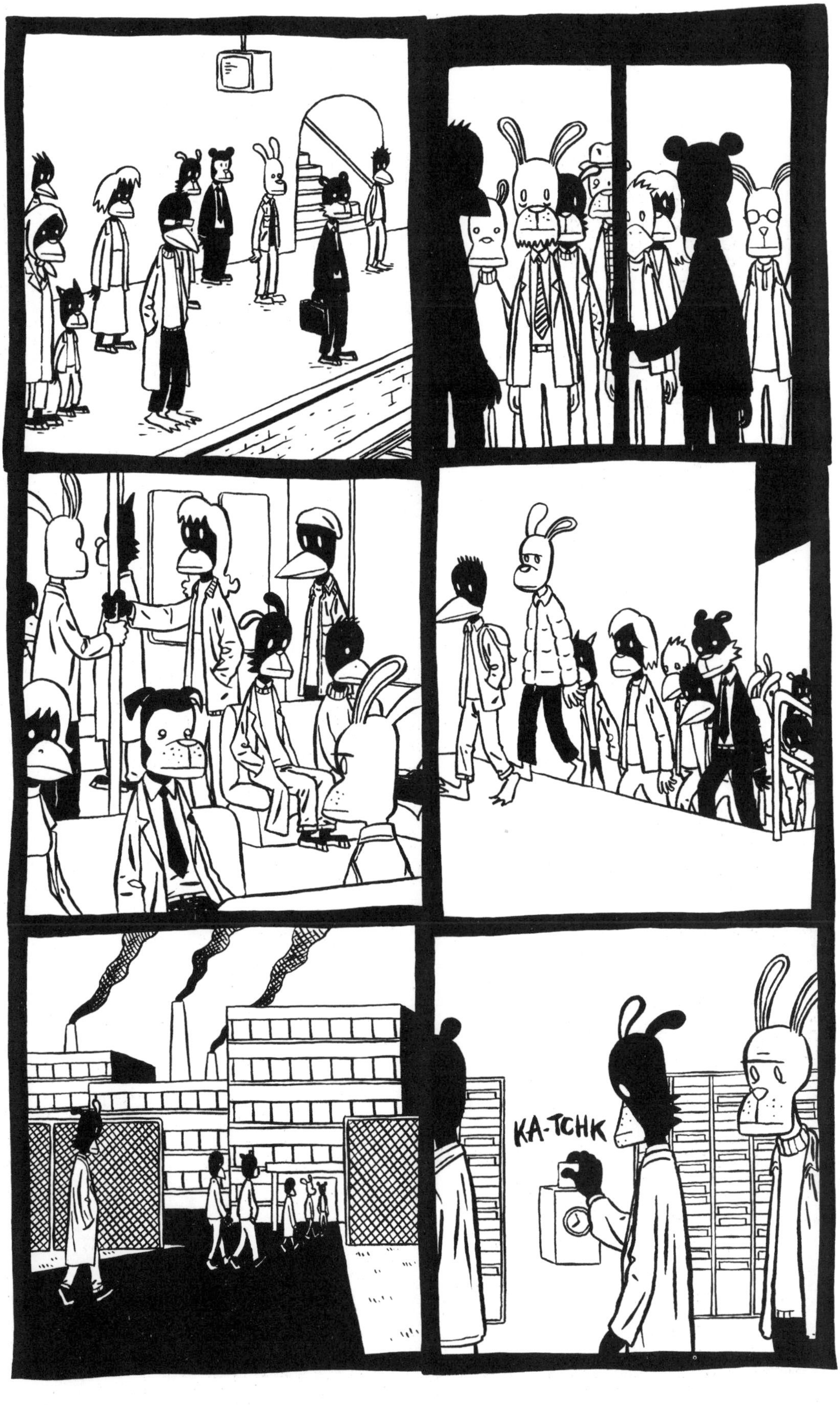
KA-TCHK

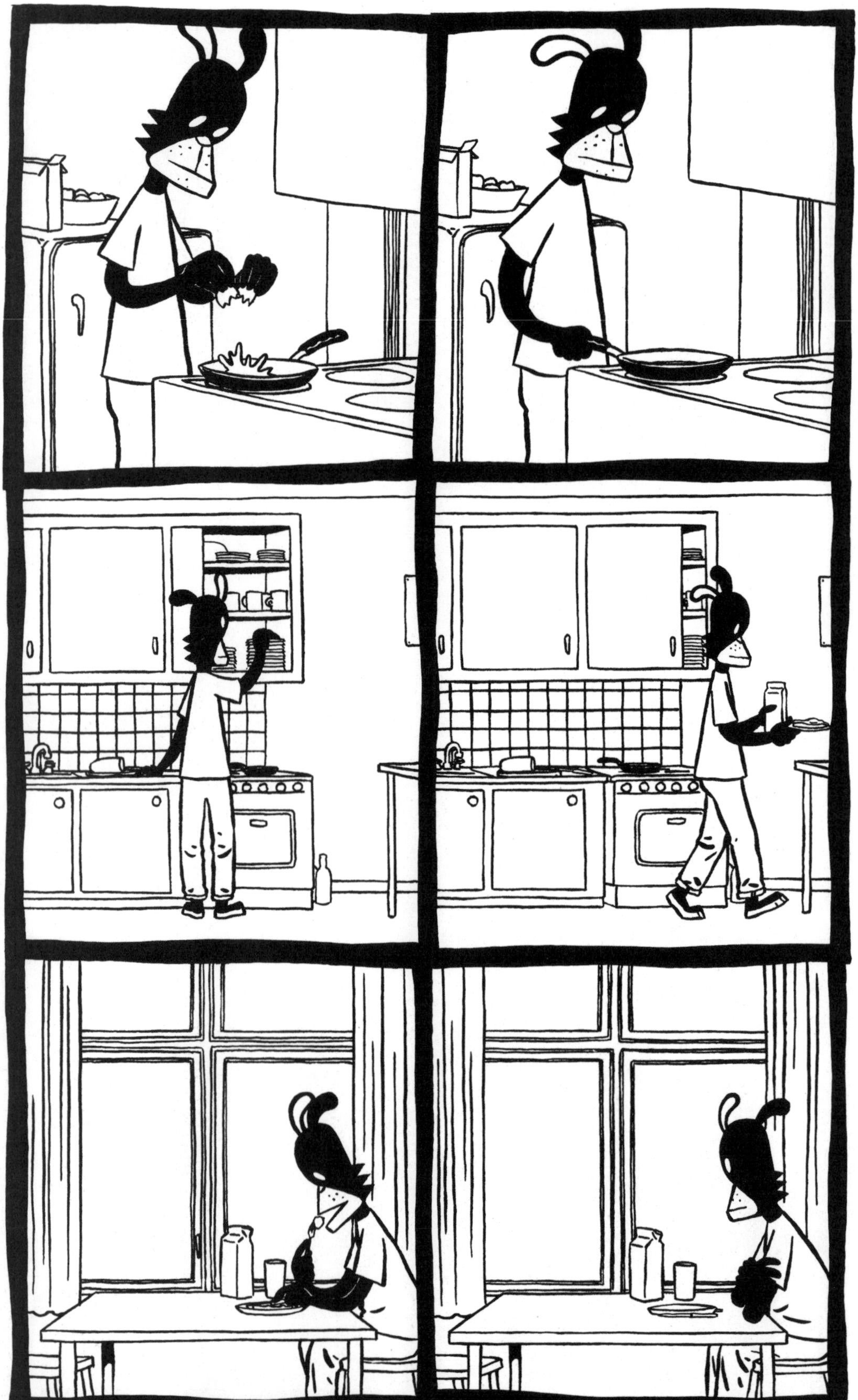

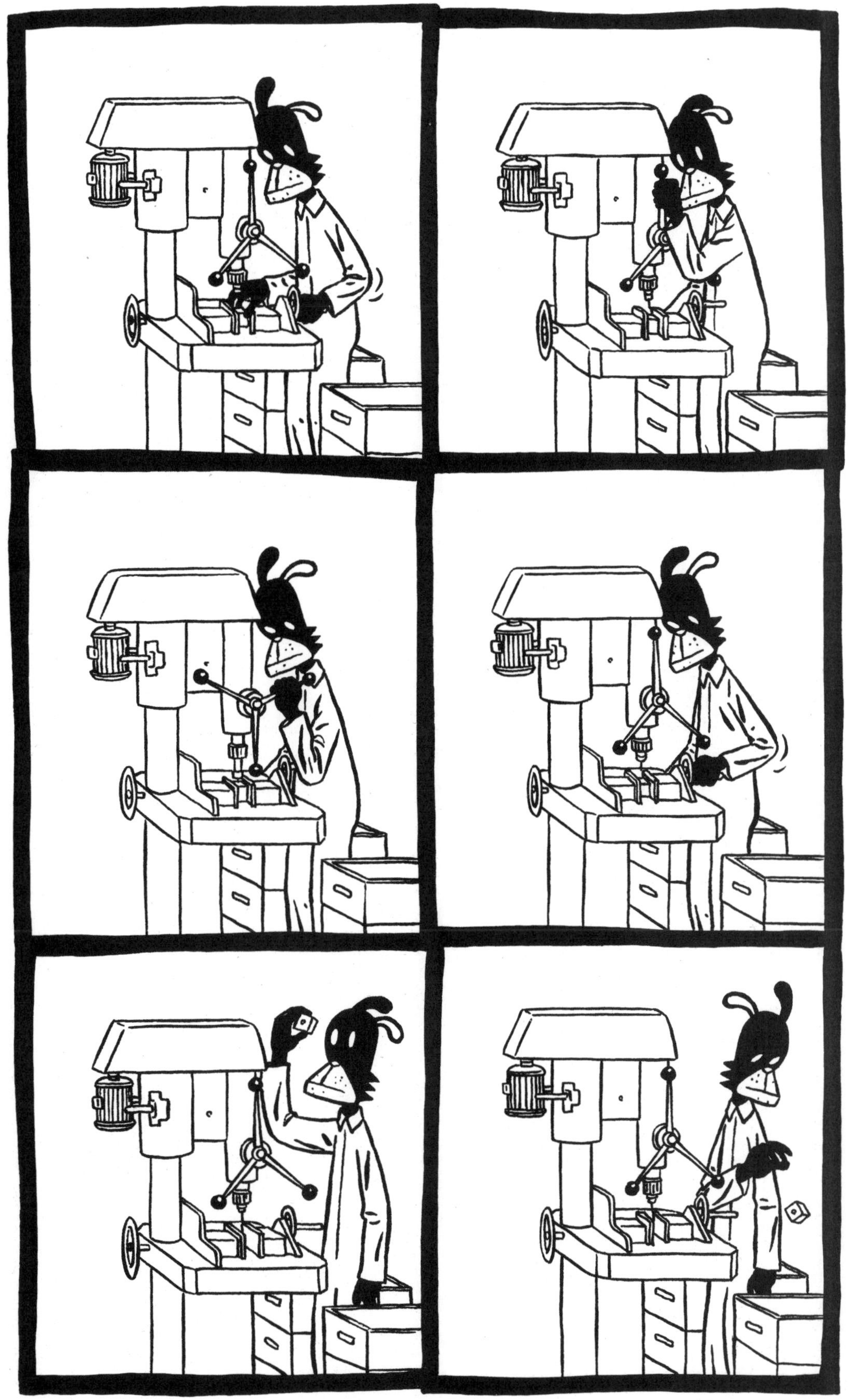

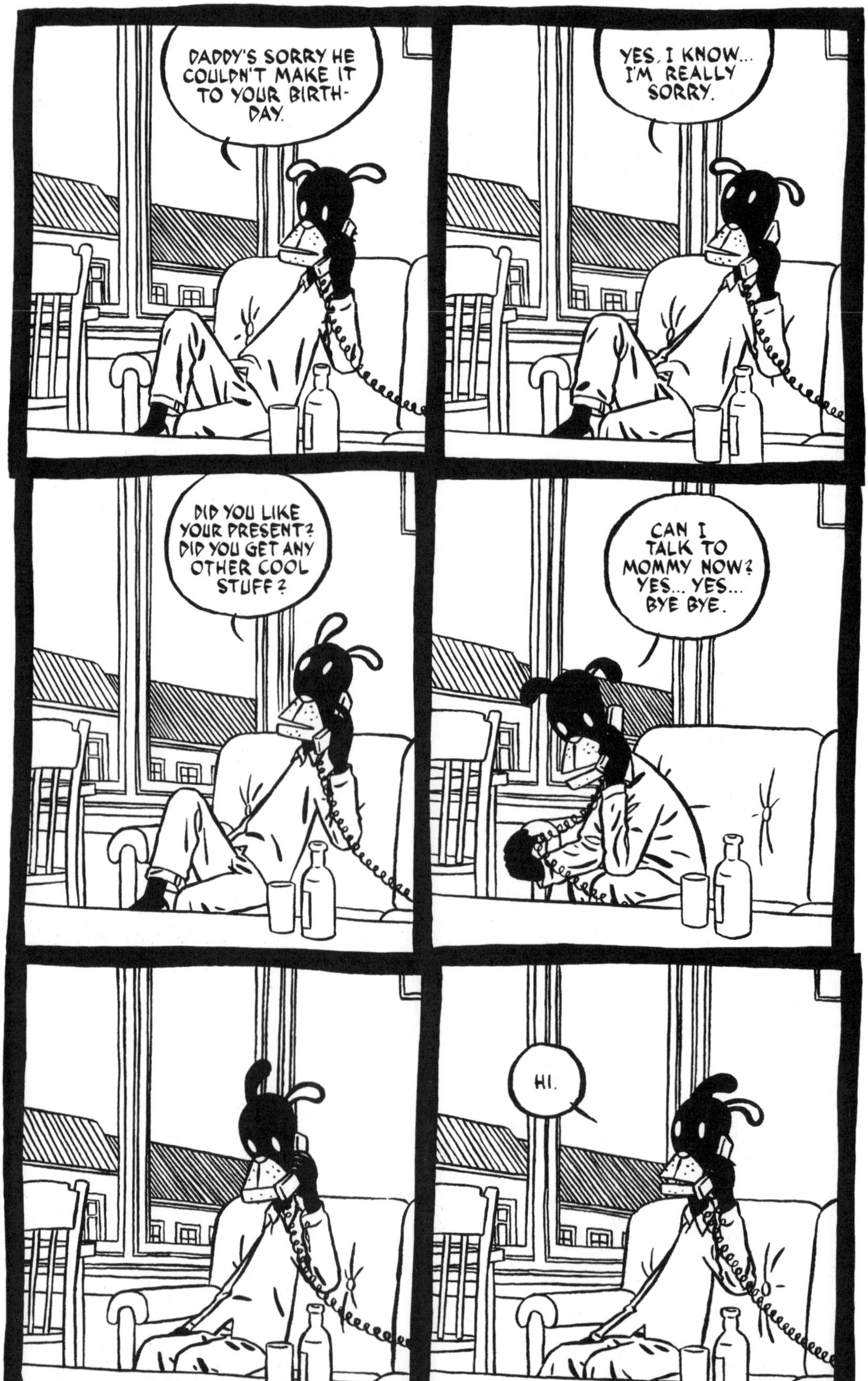
DADDY'S SORRY HE COULDN'T MAKE IT TO YOUR BIRTH-DAY.
YES, I KNOW... I'M REALLY SORRY.
DID YOU LIKE YOUR PRESENT? DID YOU GET ANY OTHER COOL STUFF?
CAN I TALK TO MOMMY NOW? YES... YES... BYE BYE.
HI.

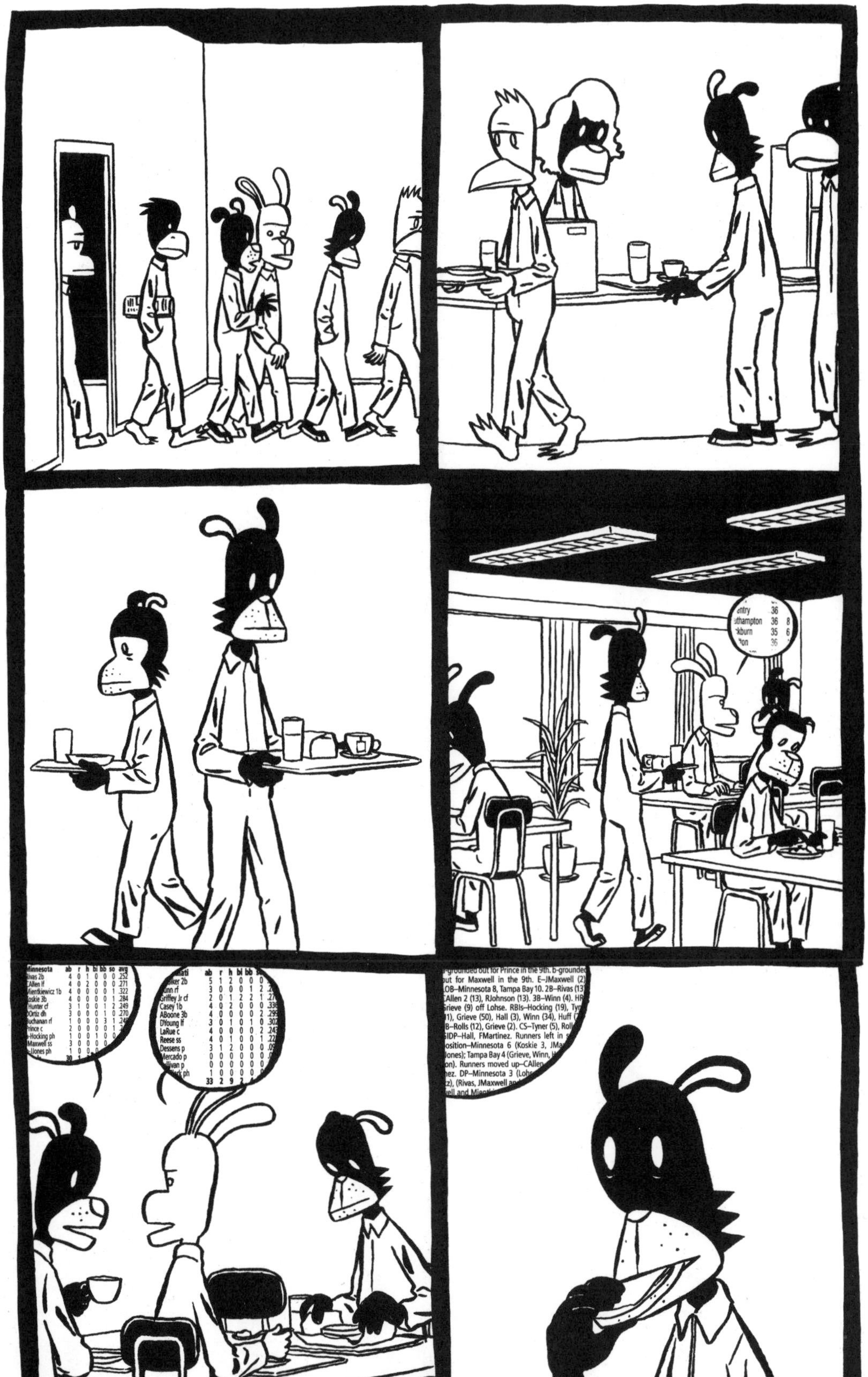

entry 36
thampton 36 8
kburn 35 6
ton 36
Minnesota ab r h bi bb so avg
Rivas 2b 4 0 1 0 0 0 .252
CAllen lf 4 0 2 0 0 0 .271
Mientkiewicz 1b 4 0 0 0 0 1 .322
Koskie 3b 4 0 0 0 0 1 .284
Hunter cf 3 1 0 0 1 2 .249
DOrtiz dh 3 0 0 0 1 0 .270
Buchanan rf 1 0 0 0 3 1
Prince c 2 0 0 0 0 1
Hocking ph 1 0 0 1 0 0
Maxwell ss 3 0 0 0 0
JJones ph 1 0
ab r h bi bb
Casey 1b 4 0 2 0 0 0 .336
ABoone 3b 4 0 0 0 0 2
DYoung lf 3 0 1 0 1 0
LaRue c 4 0 0 0 0 2
Reese ss 4 0 1 0 0 1
Dessens p 3 1 2 0 0 0
Mercado p 0 0 0 0 0 0
33 2 9
out for Maxwell in the 9th. E–JMaxwell (2)
OB–Minnesota 8, Tampa Bay 10. 2B–Rivas (13)
CAllen 2 (13), RJohnson (13). 3B–Winn (4).
rieve (9) off Lohse. RBIs–Hocking (19),
1), Grieve (50), Hall (3), Winn (34), Huff
B–Rolls (12), Grieve (2). CS–Tyner (5),
IDP–Hall, FMartinez. Runners left in
osition–Minnesota 6 (Koskie 3,
ones); Tampa Bay 4 (Grieve, Winn,
on). Runners moved up–
ez. DP–Minnesota 3
z), (Rivas, JMaxwell

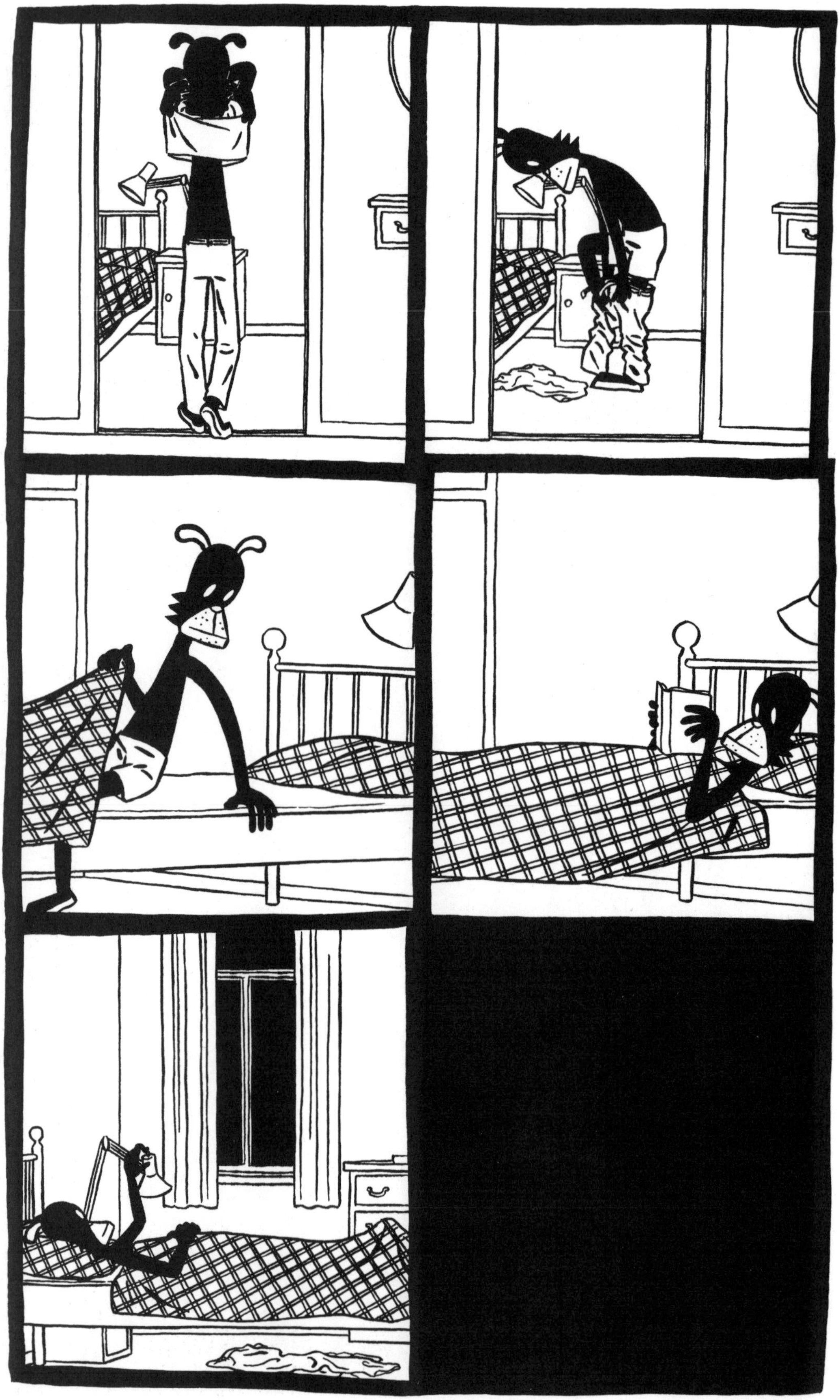

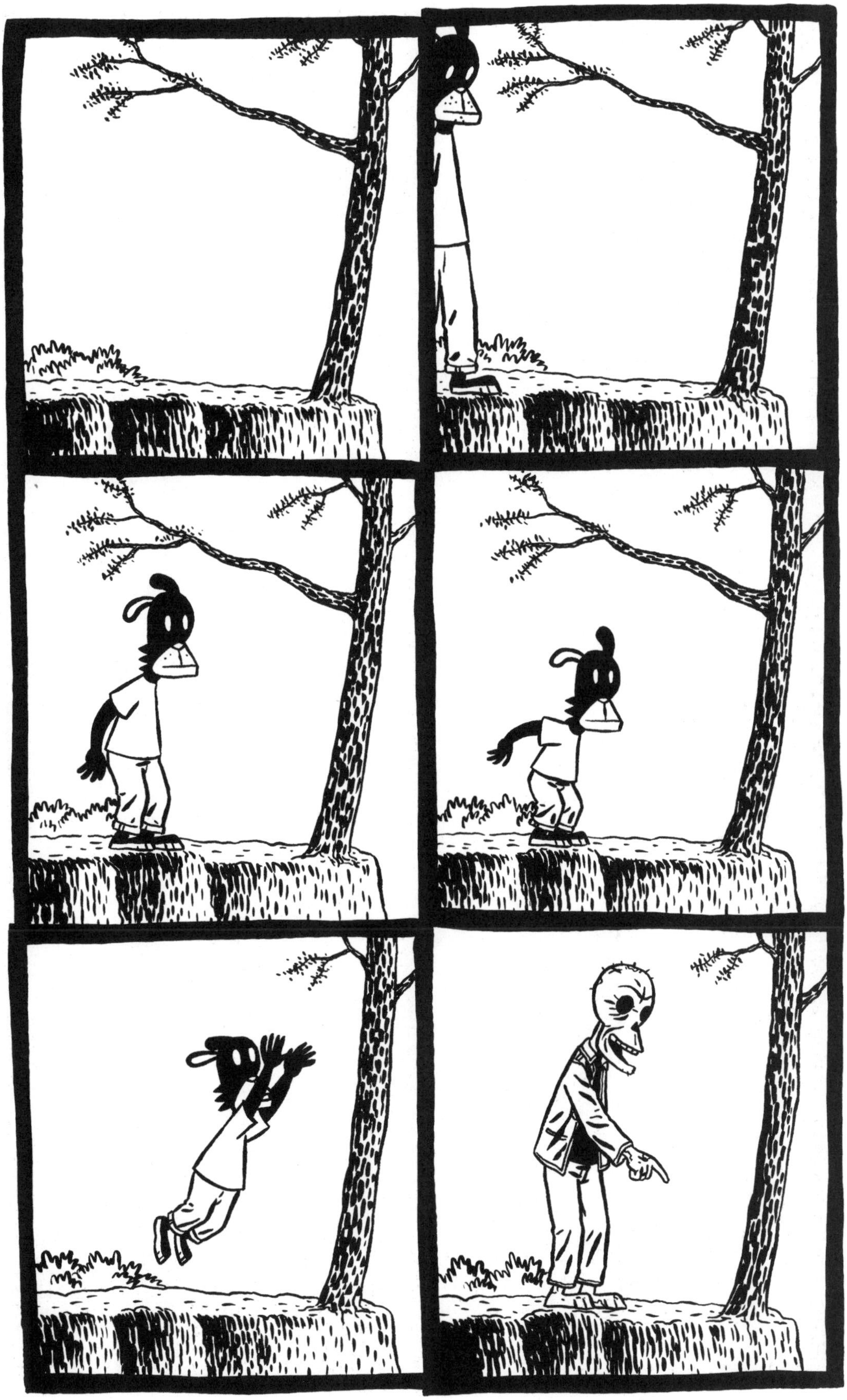

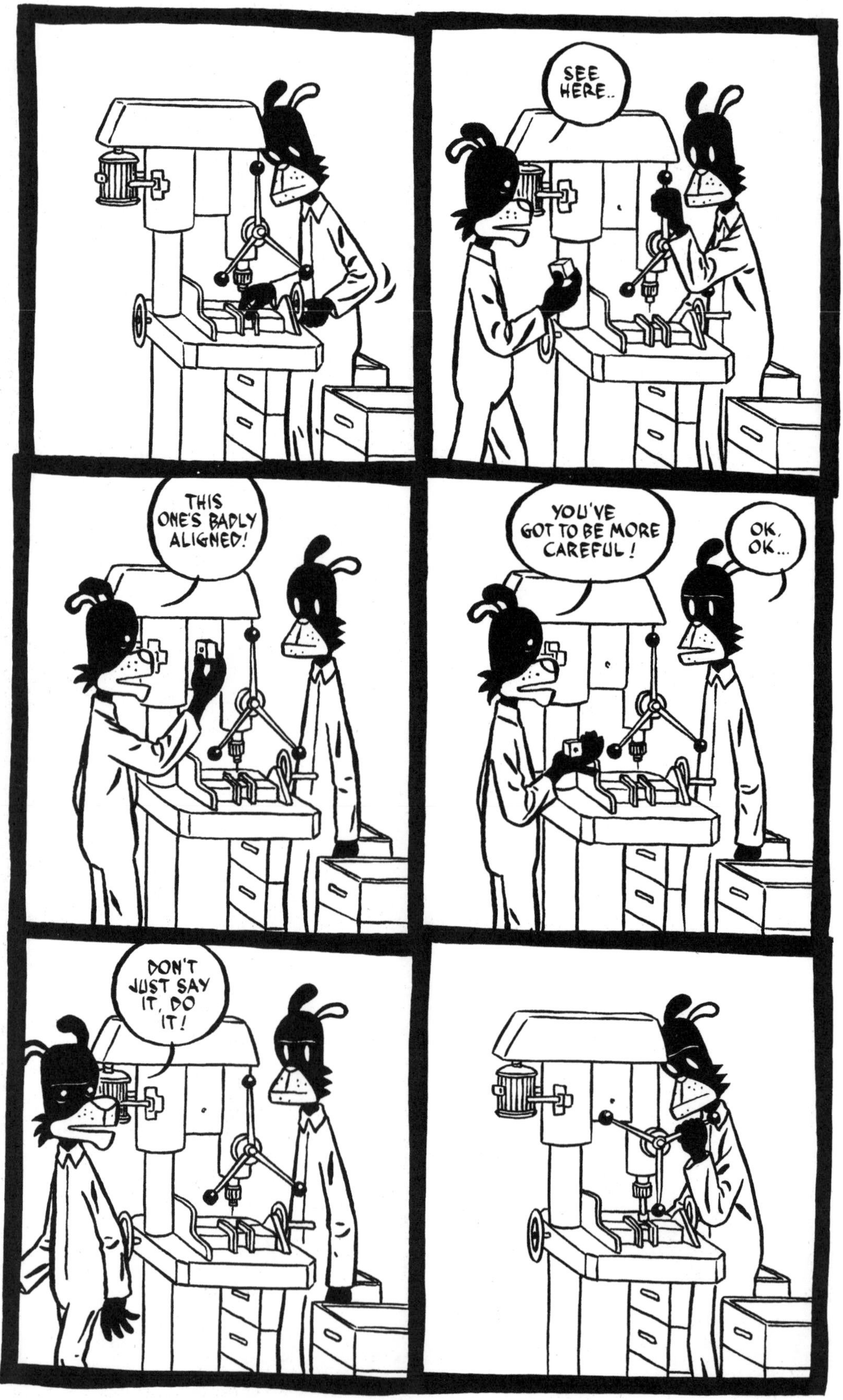
SEE HERE..
THIS ONE'S BADLY ALIGNED!
YOU'VE GOT TO BE MORE CAREFUL!
OK, OK...
DON'T JUST SAY IT, DO IT!

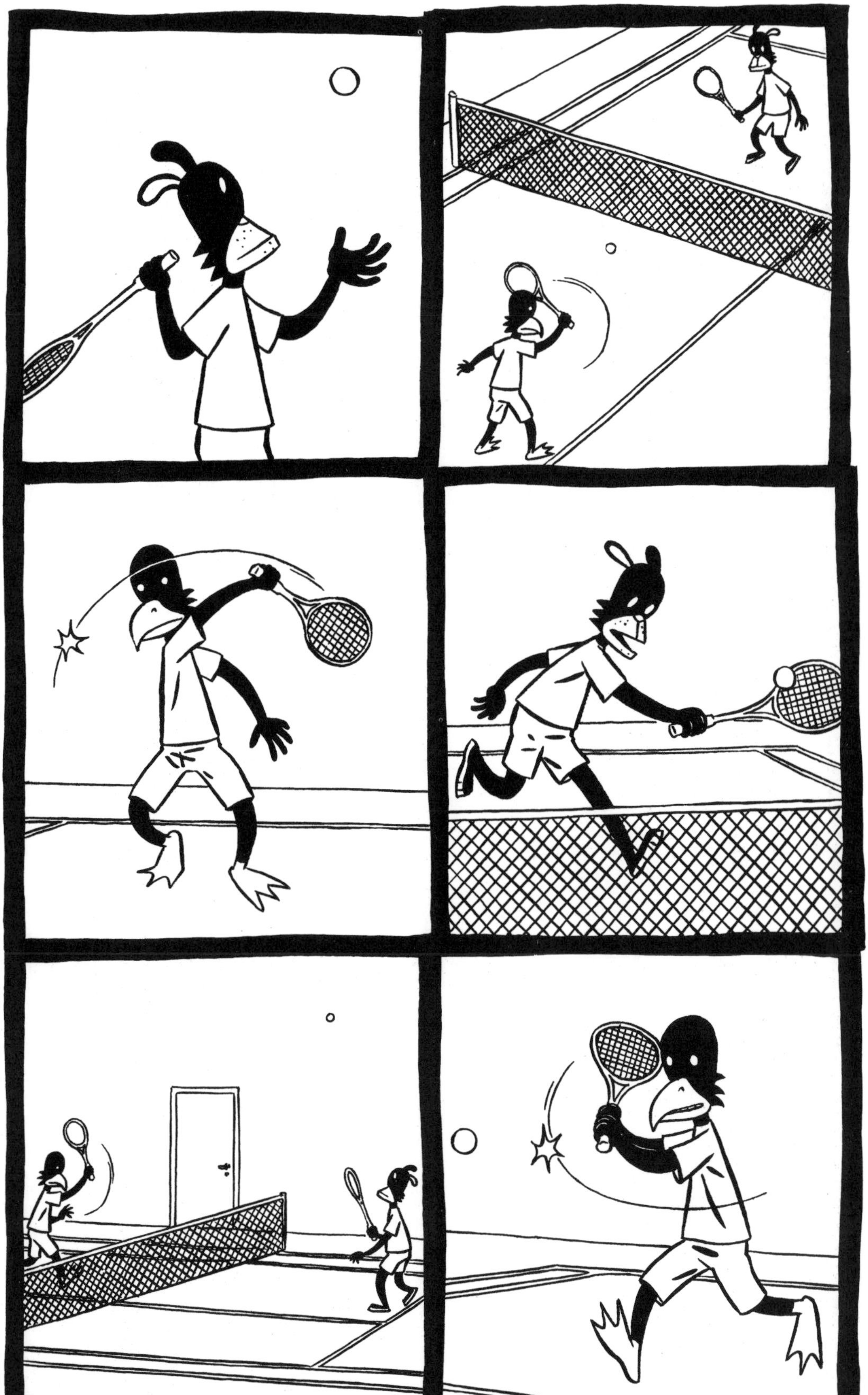

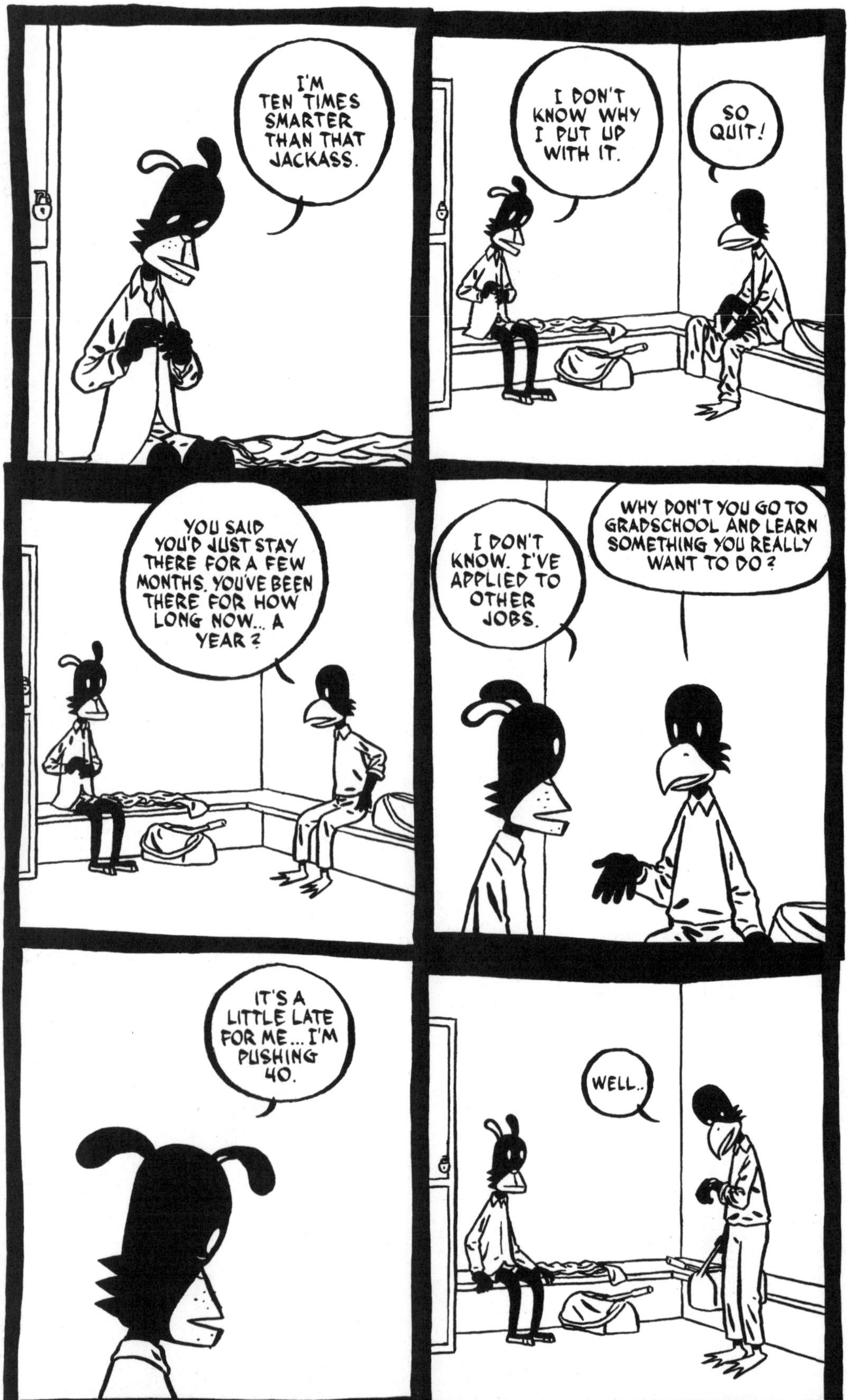
I'M TEN TIMES SMARTER THAN THAT JACKASS.
I DON'T KNOW WHY I PUT UP WITH IT.
SO QUIT!
YOU SAID YOU'D JUST STAY THERE FOR A FEW MONTHS. YOU'VE BEEN THERE FOR HOW LONG NOW... A YEAR?
WHY DON'T YOU GO TO GRADSCHOOL AND LEARN SOMETHING YOU REALLY WANT TO DO?
I DON'T KNOW. I'VE APPLIED TO OTHER JOBS.
IT'S A LITTLE LATE FOR ME... I'M PUSHING 40.
WELL..

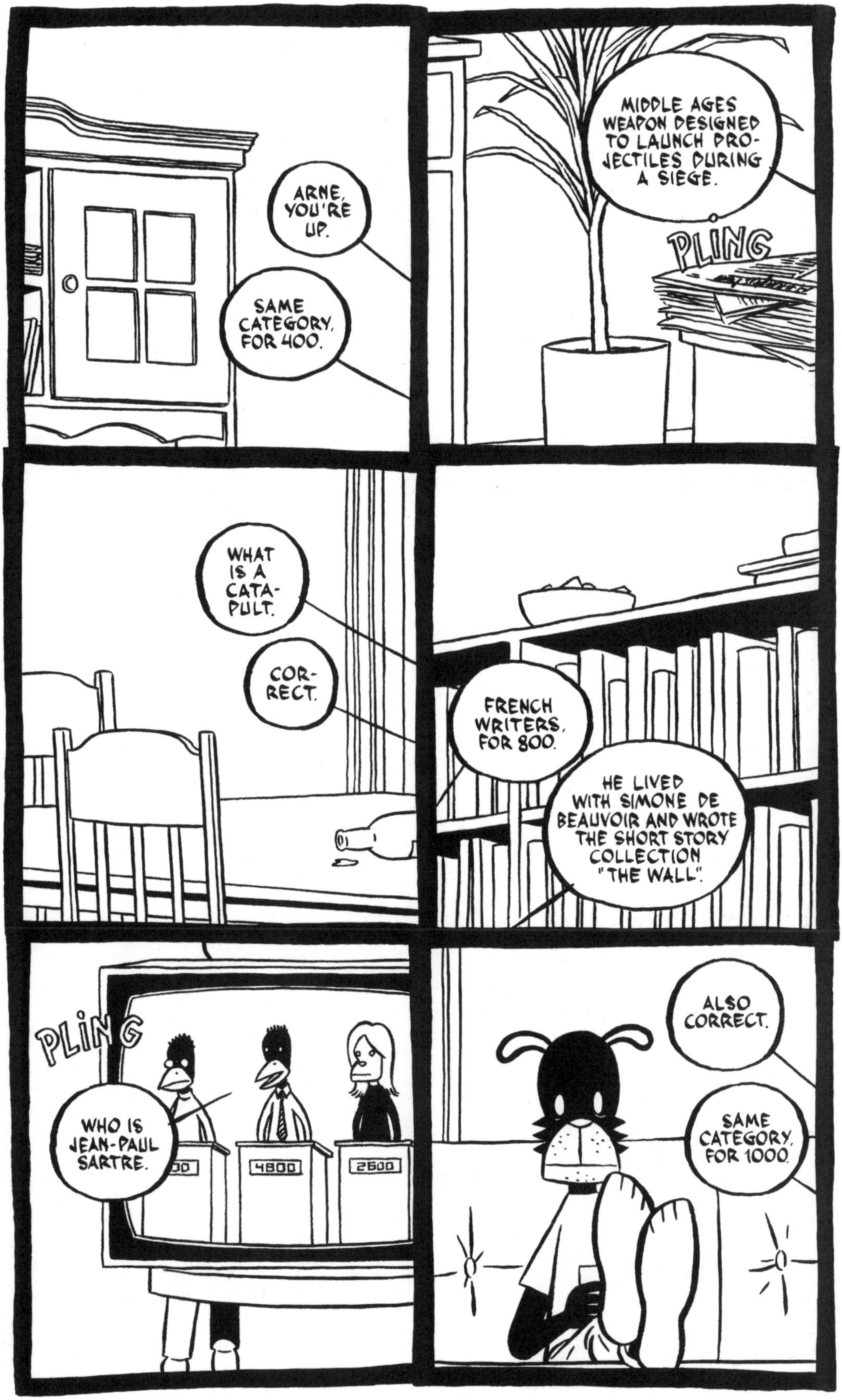
ARNE, YOU'RE UP.
SAME CATEGORY, FOR 400.
MIDDLE AGES WEAPON DESIGNED TO LAUNCH PROJECTILES DURING A SIEGE.
PLING
WHAT IS A CATAPULT.
CORRECT.
FRENCH WRITERS, FOR 800.
HE LIVED WITH SIMONE DE BEAUVOIR AND WROTE THE SHORT STORY COLLECTION "THE WALL".
PLING
WHO IS JEAN-PAUL SARTRE.
4800
2600
ALSO CORRECT.
SAME CATEGORY, FOR 1000.

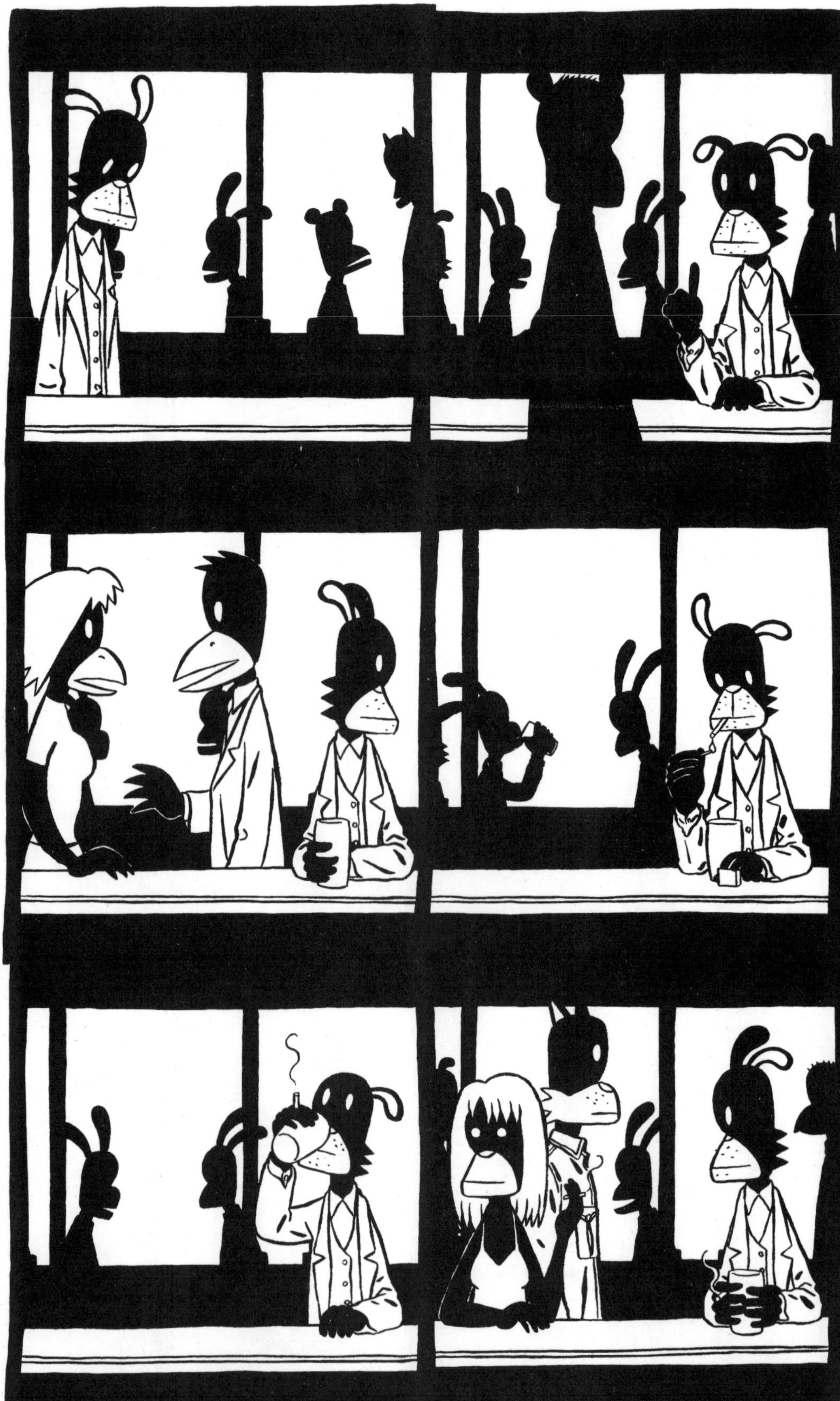

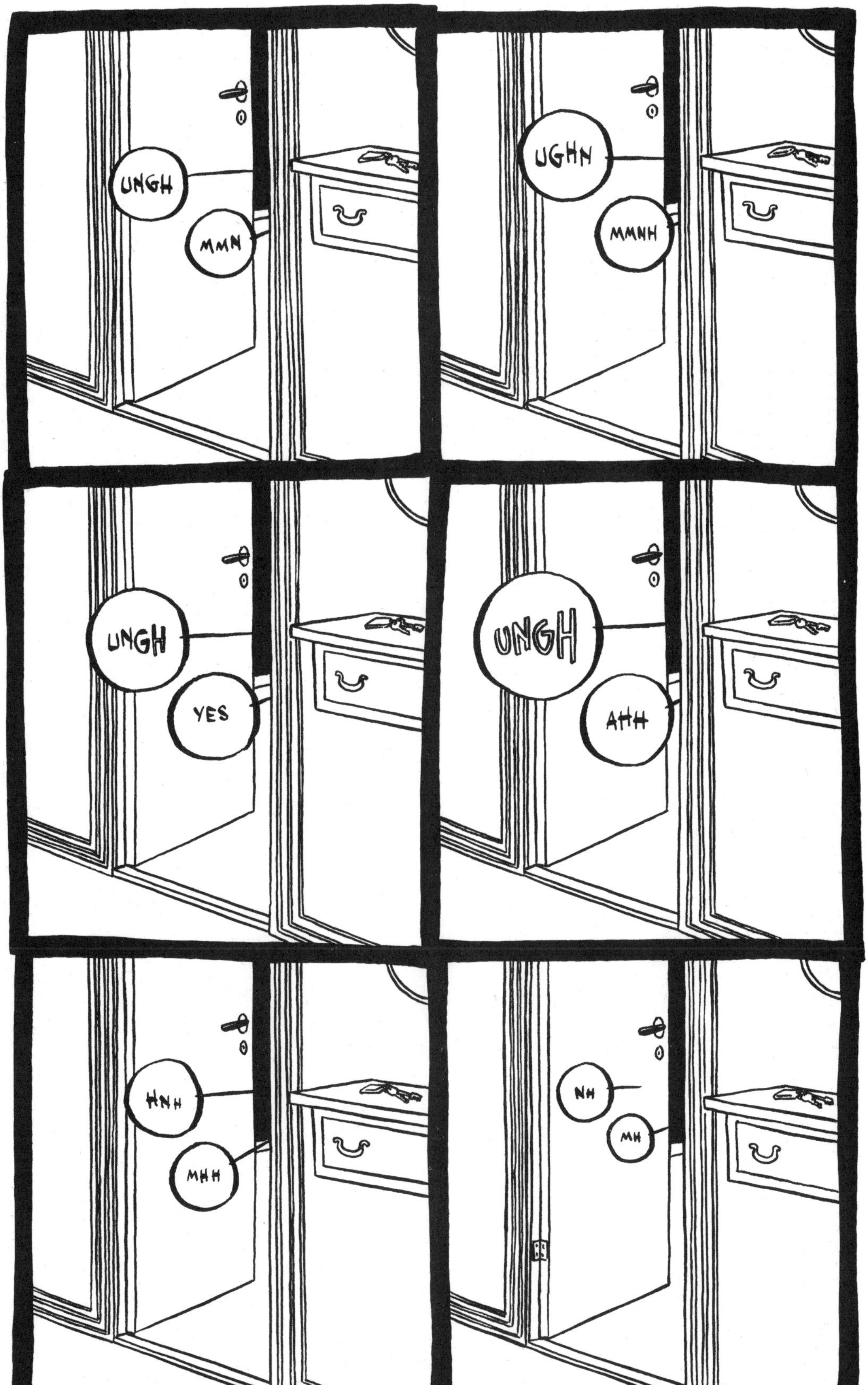
UNGH
MMN
UGHN
MMNH
UNGH
YES
UNGH
AHH
HNH
MHH
NH
MH

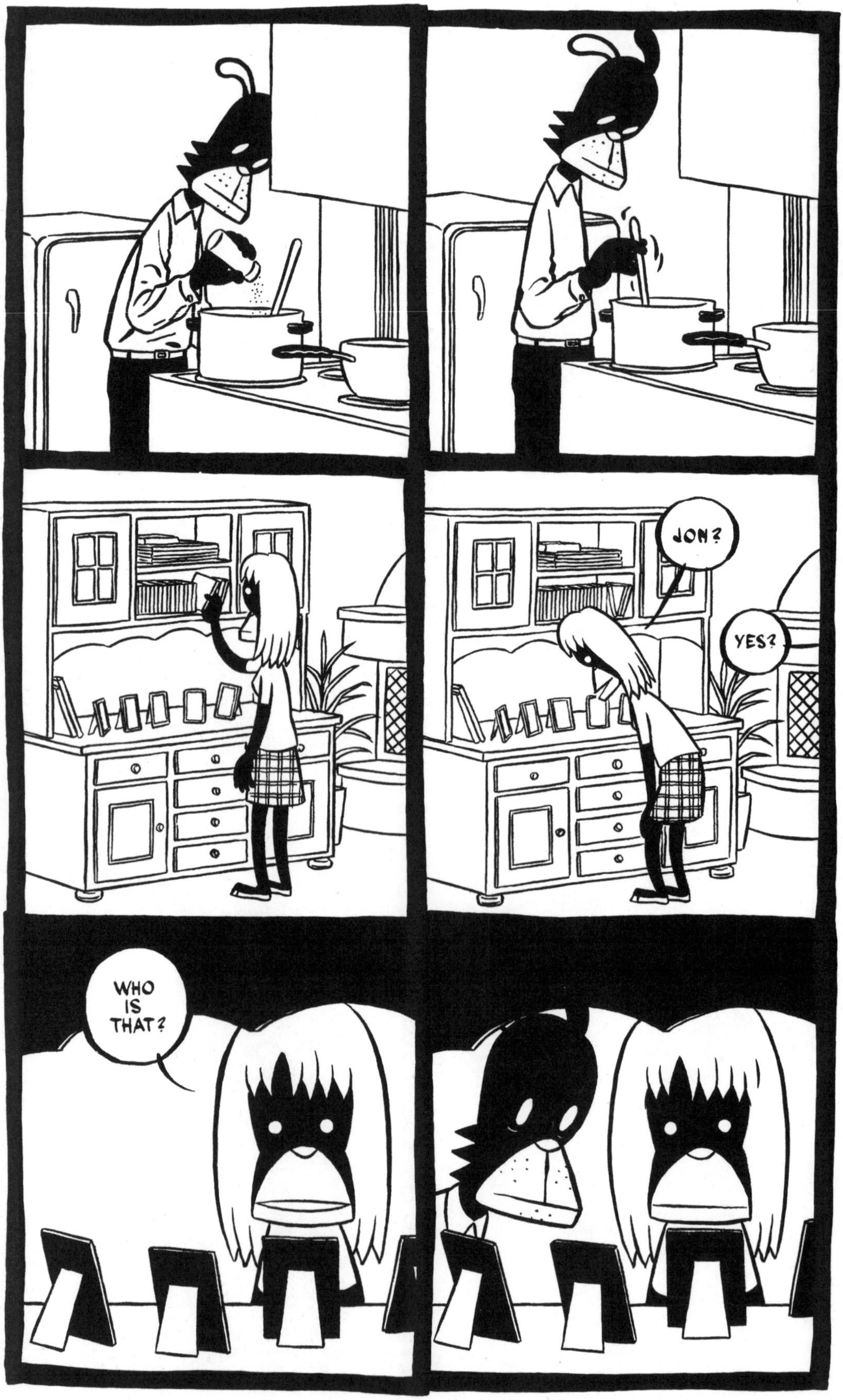
JON?
YES?
WHO IS THAT?

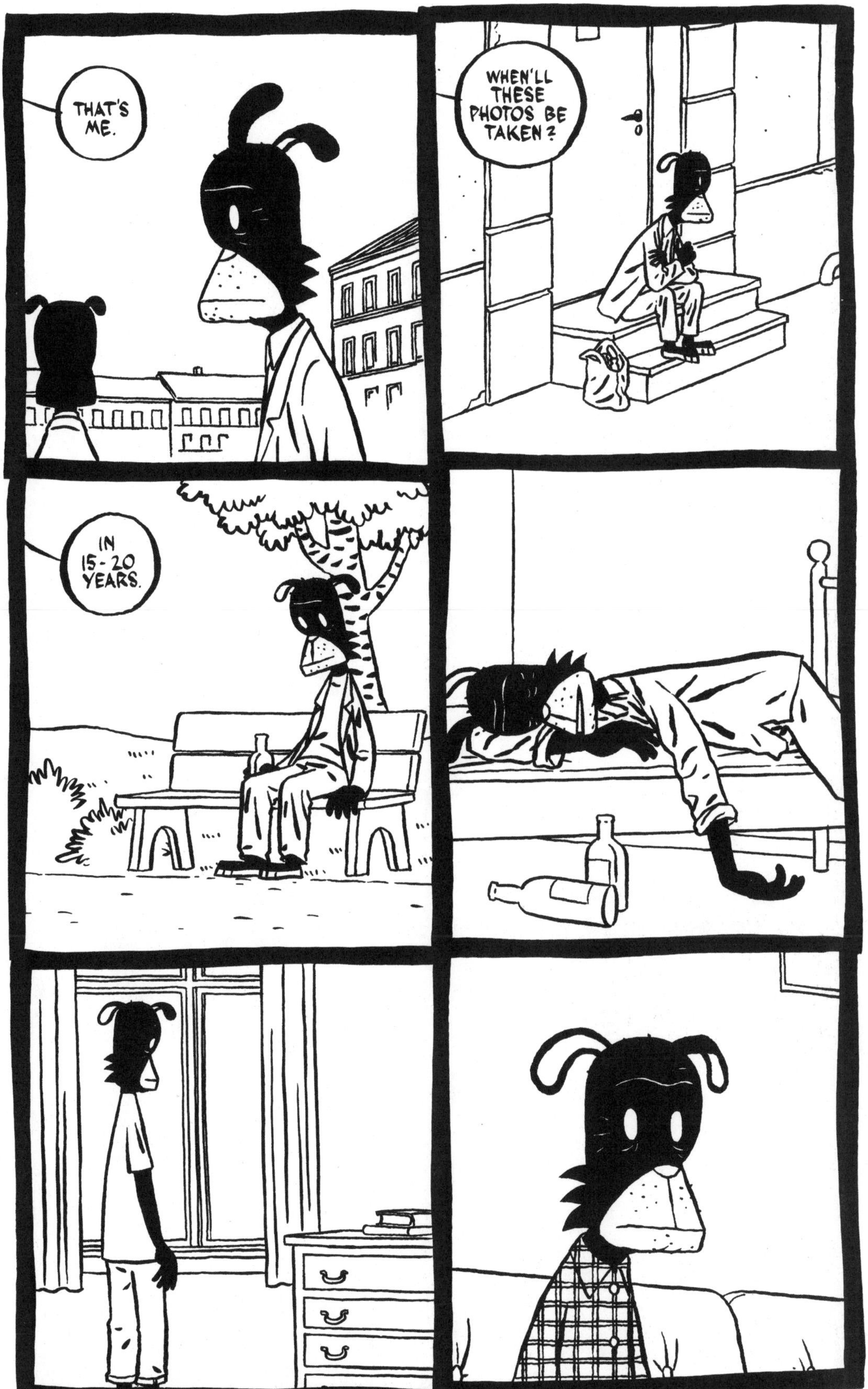
THAT'S ME.
WHEN'LL THESE PHOTOS BE TAKEN?
IN 15-20 YEARS.

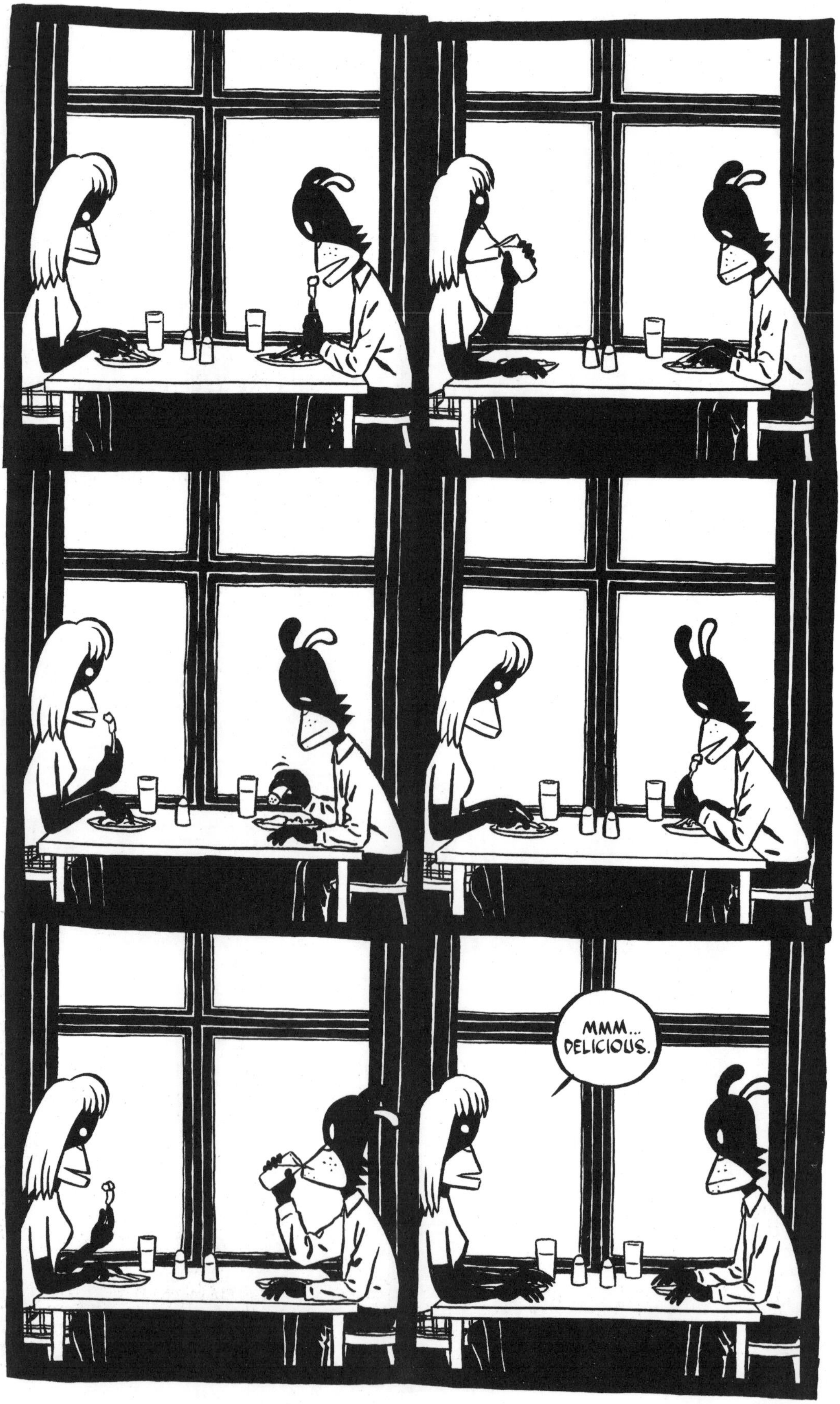
MMM... DELICIOUS.

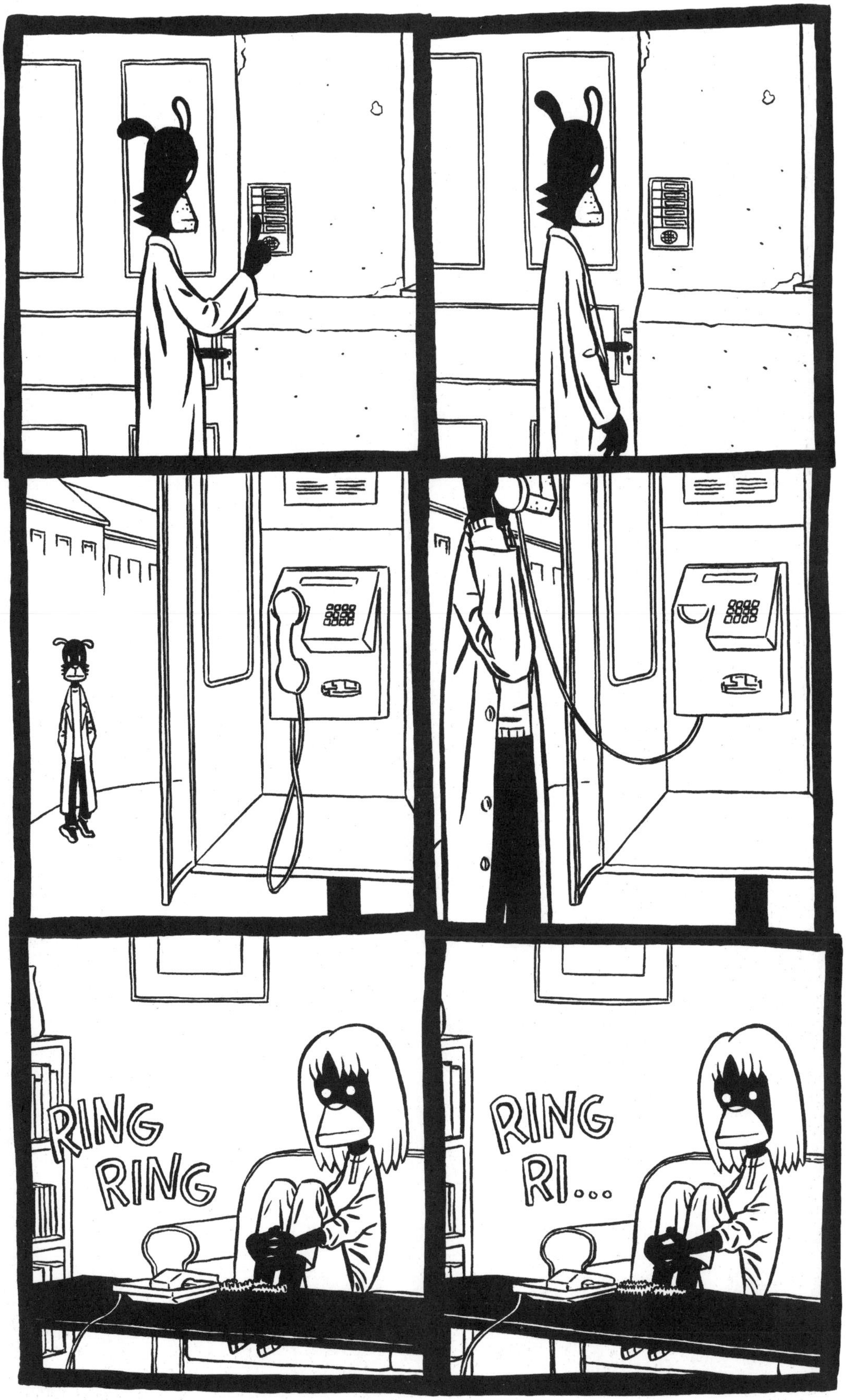
RING
RING
RING
RI...

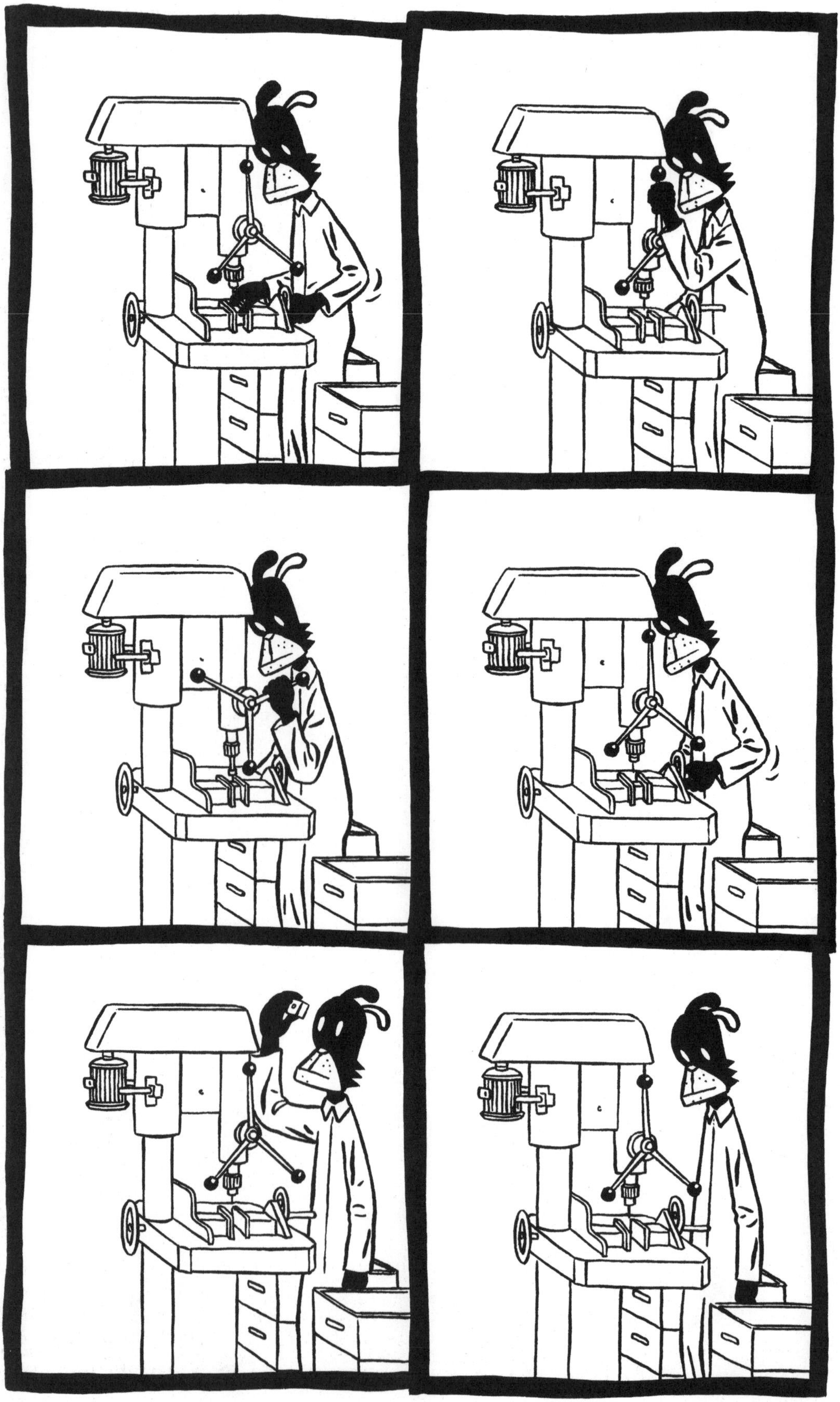

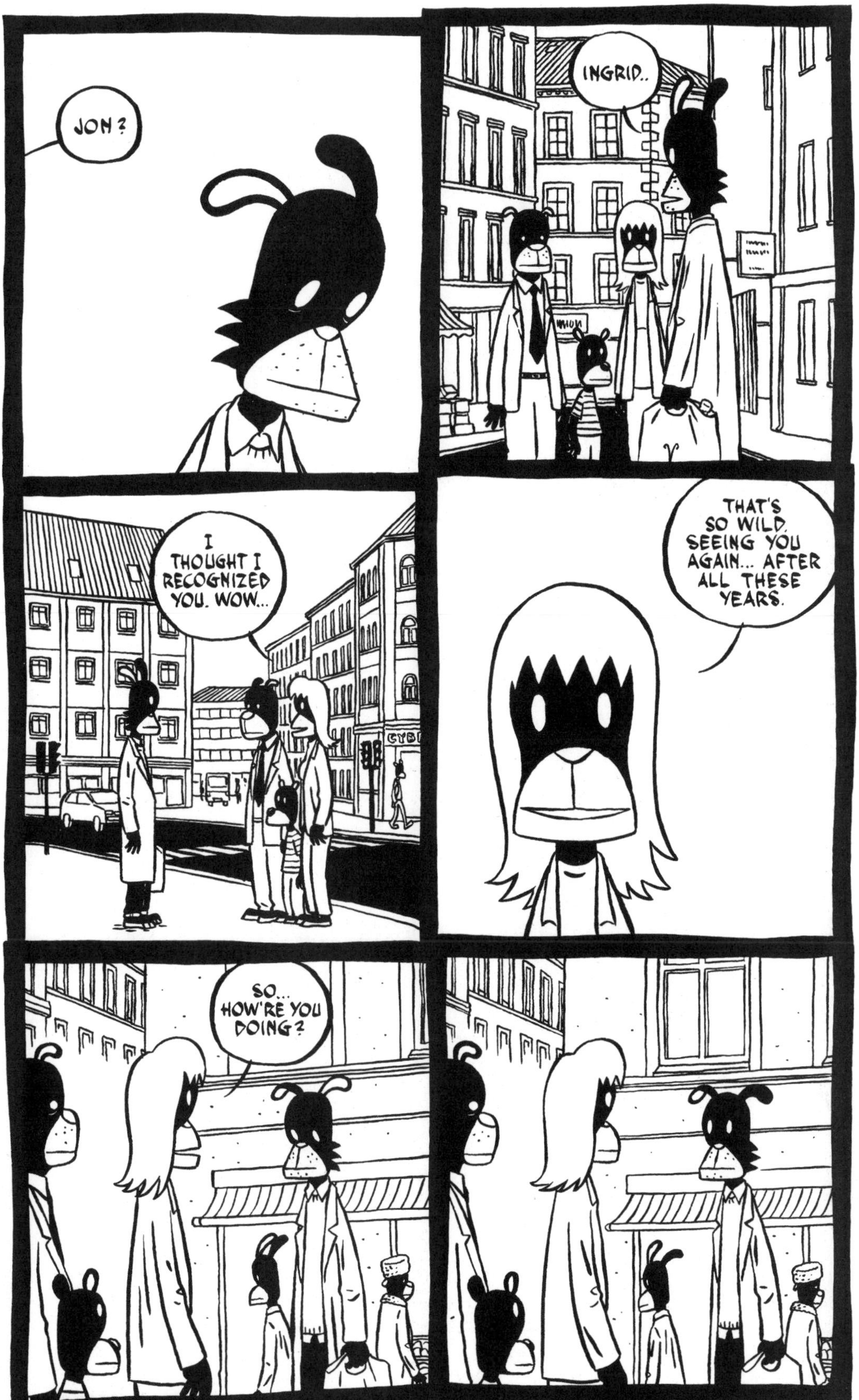
JON?
INGRID..
I THOUGHT I RECOGNIZED YOU. WOW...
THAT'S SO WILD. SEEING YOU AGAIN... AFTER ALL THESE YEARS.
SO... HOW'RE YOU DOING?

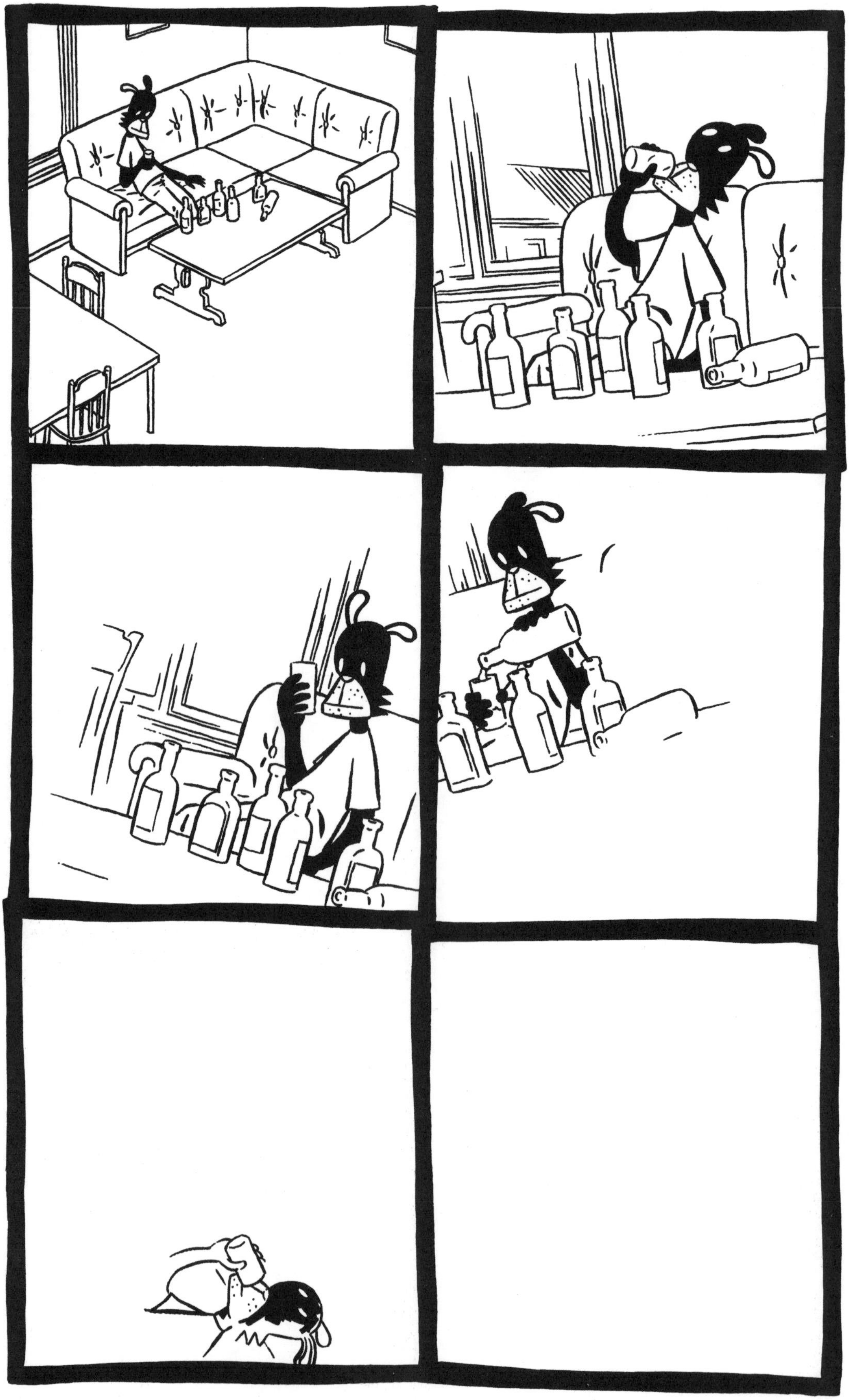

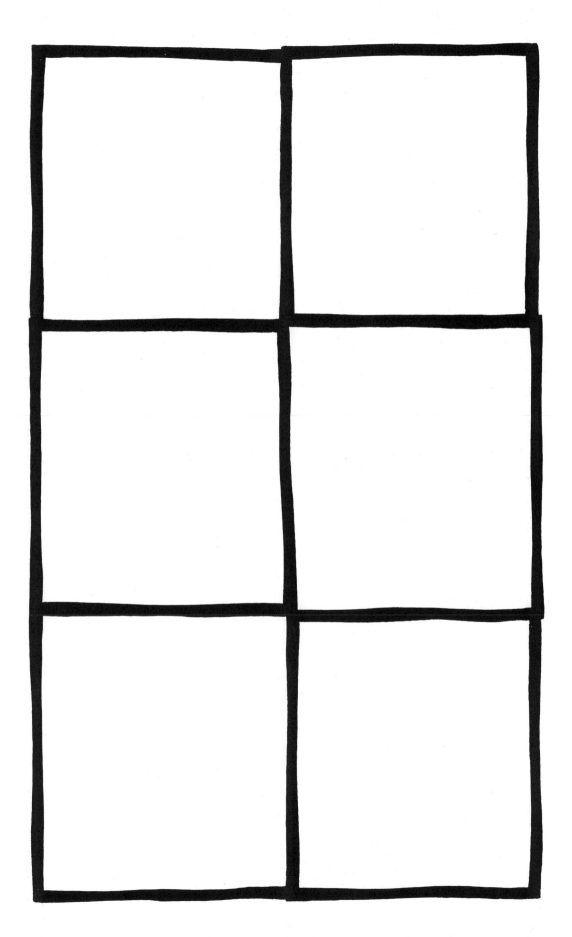

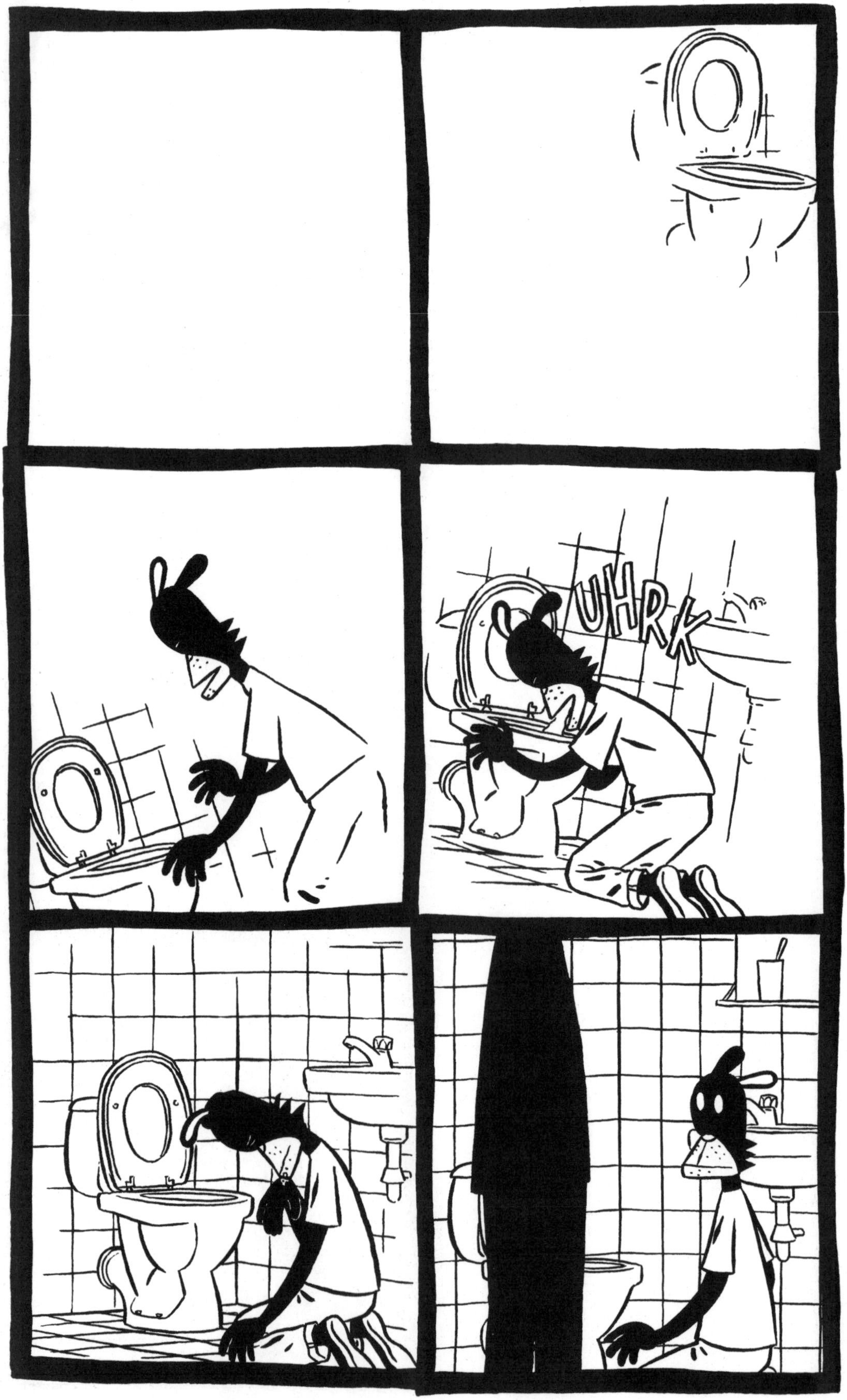
UHRK

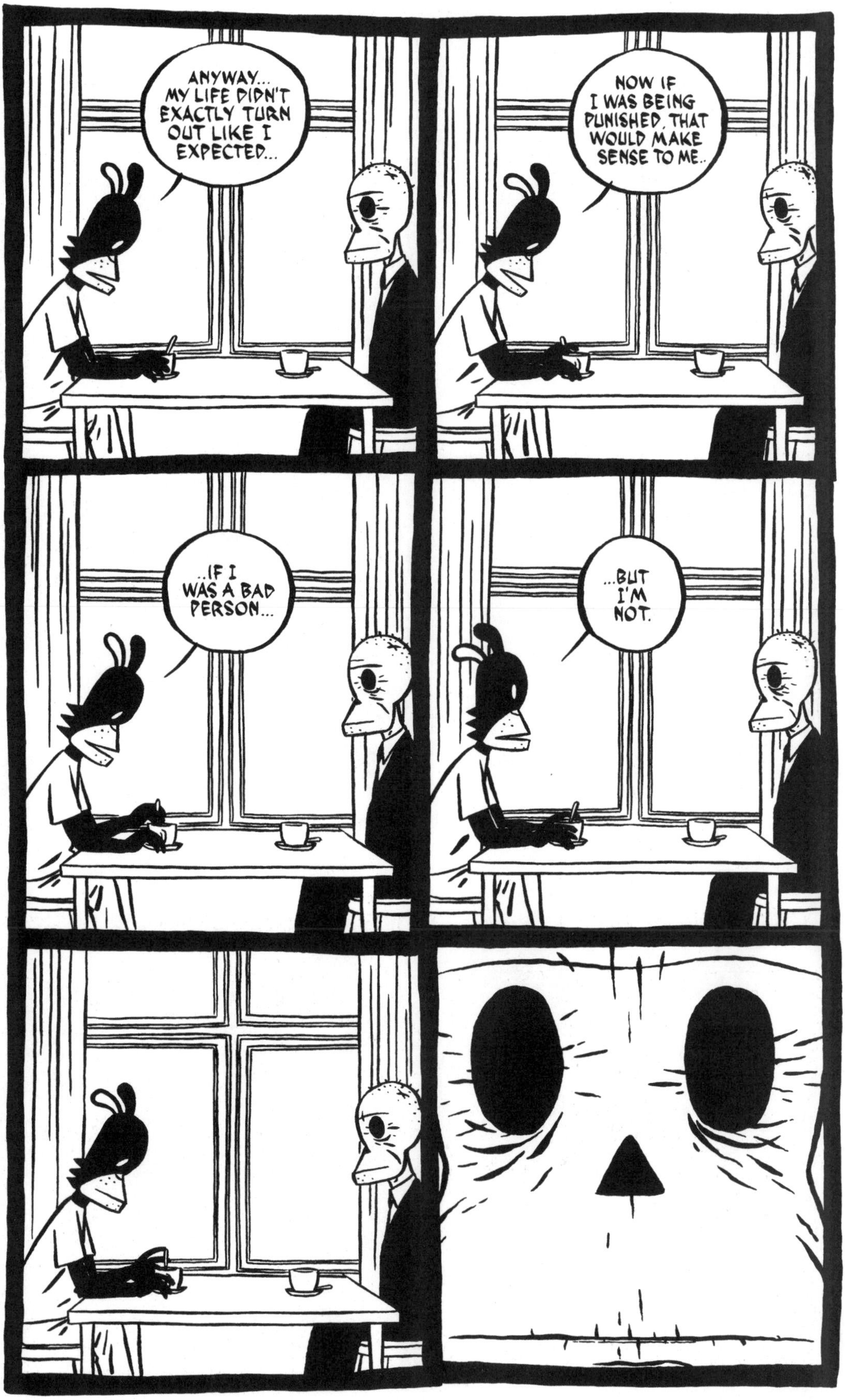
ANYWAY... MY LIFE DIDN'T EXACTLY TURN OUT LIKE I EXPECTED...
NOW IF I WAS BEING PUNISHED, THAT WOULD MAKE SENSE TO ME..
...IF I WAS A BAD PERSON...
...BUT I'M NOT.

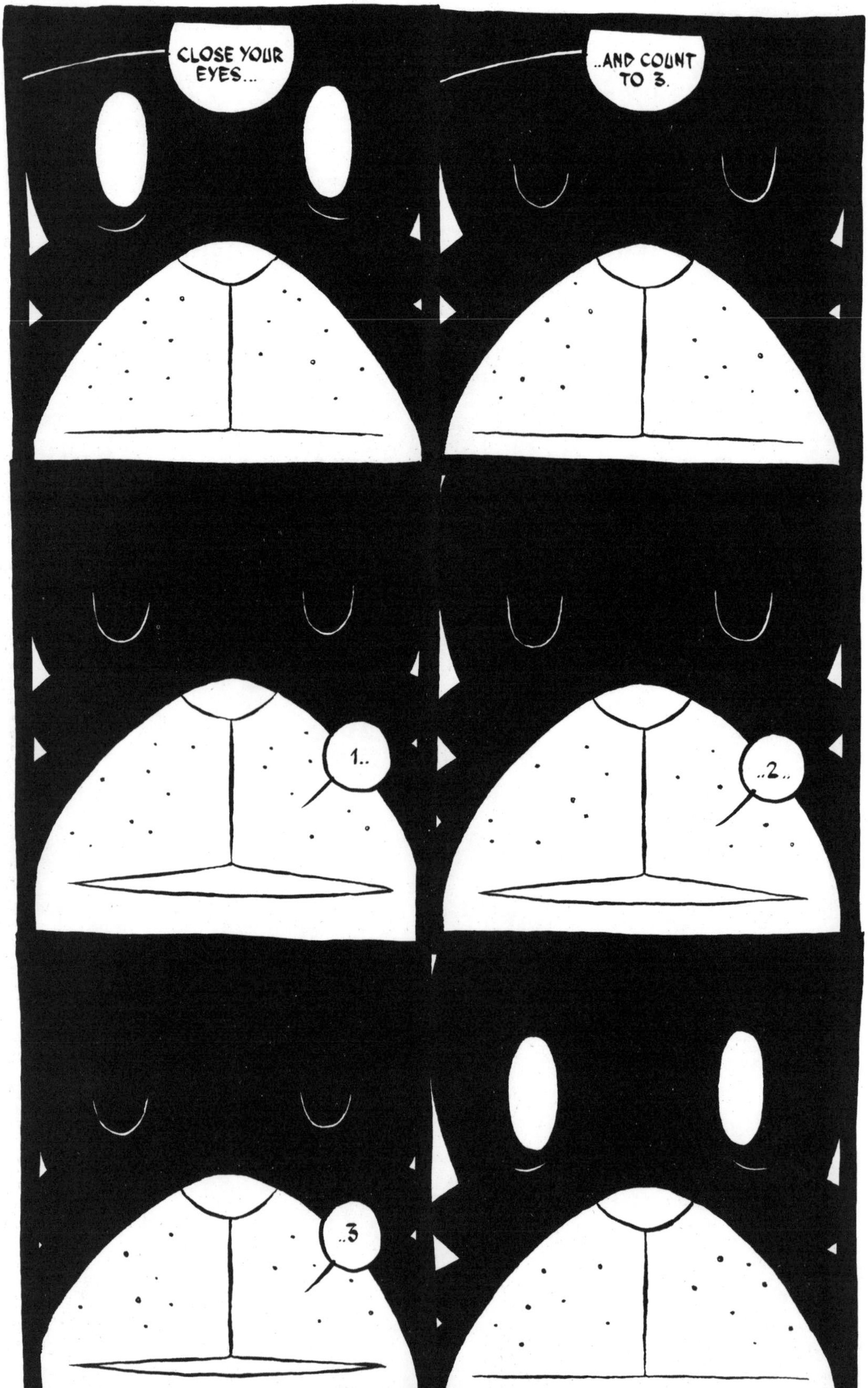
CLOSE YOUR EYES...
..AND COUNT TO 3.
1..
..2..
..3

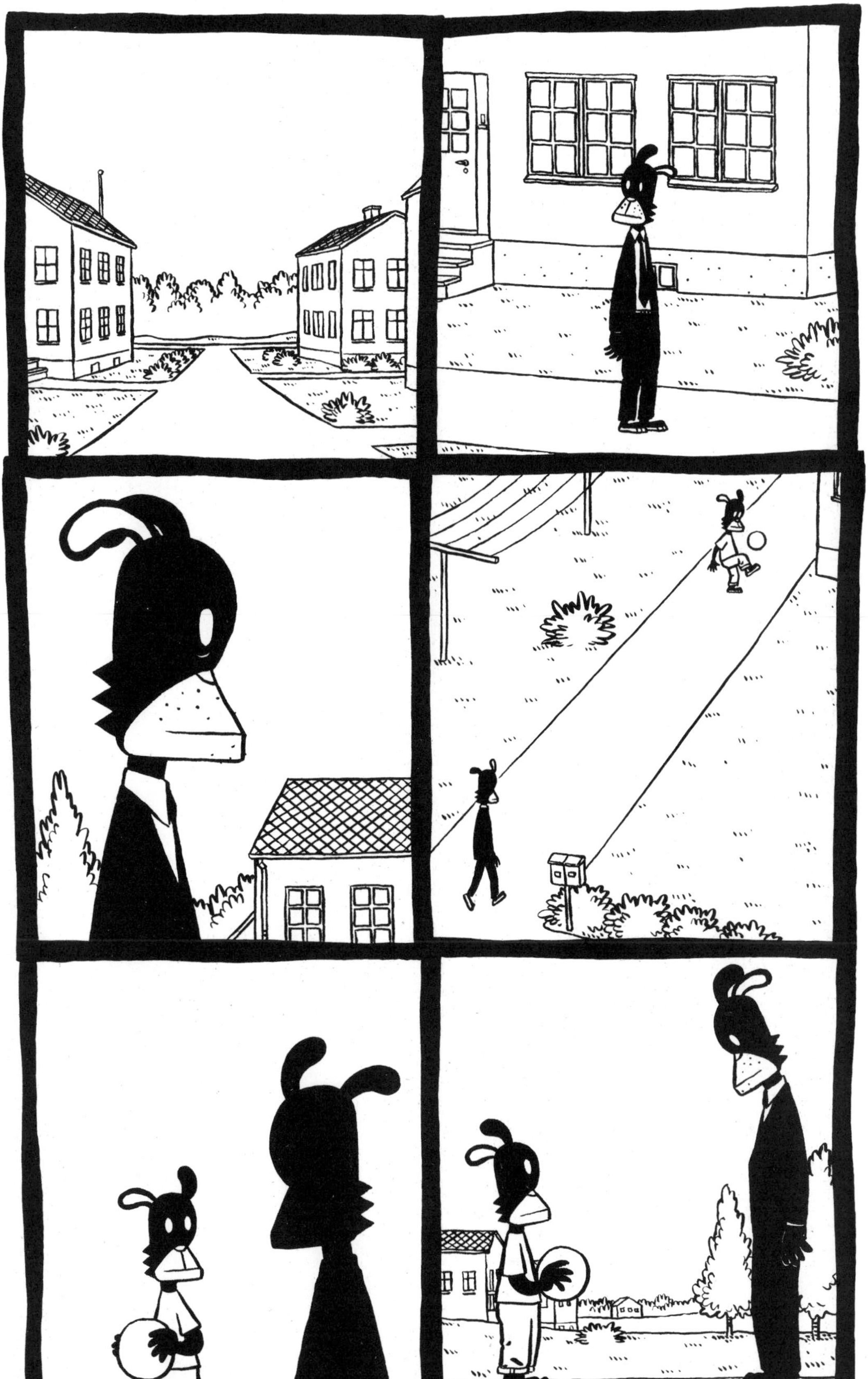

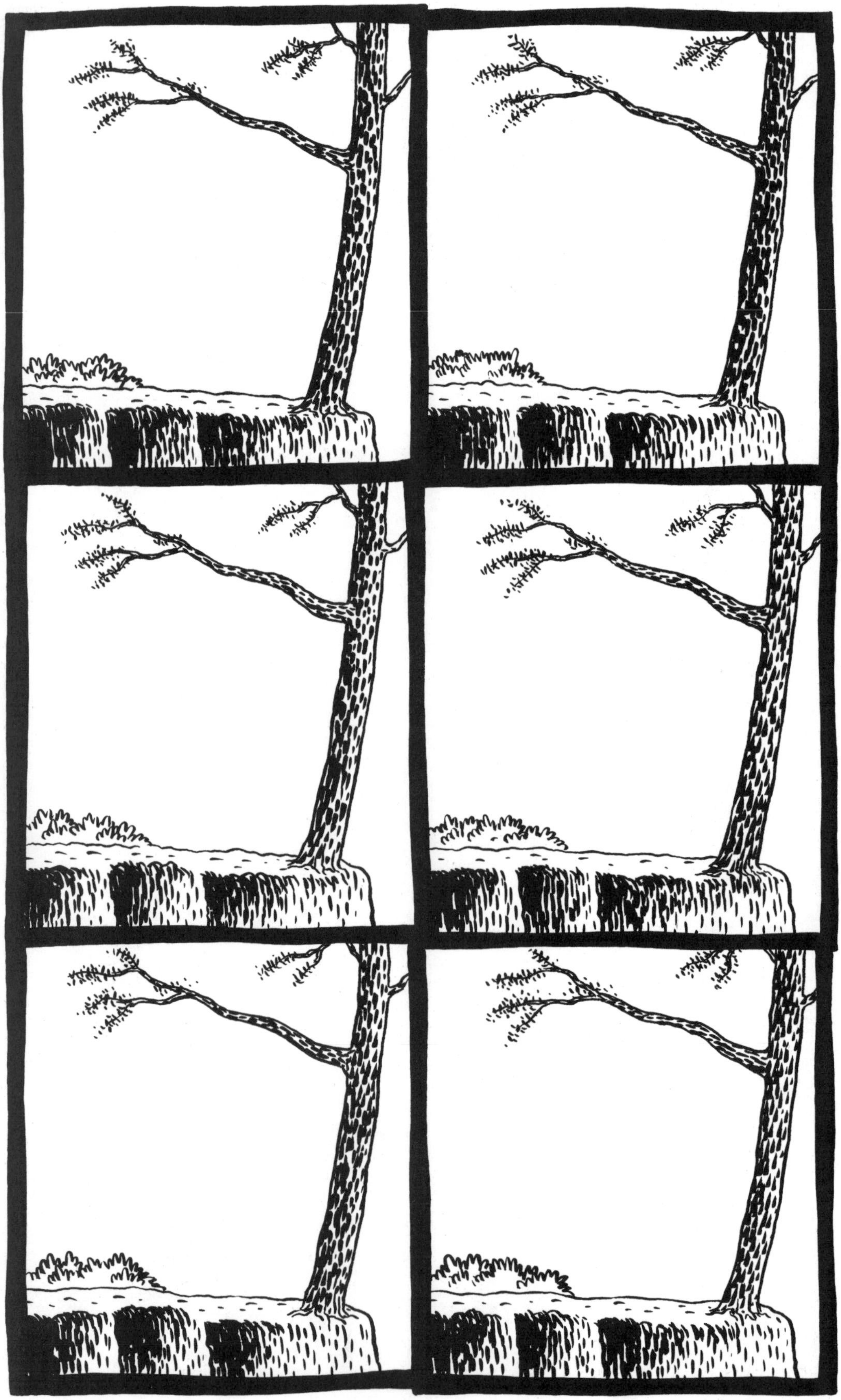

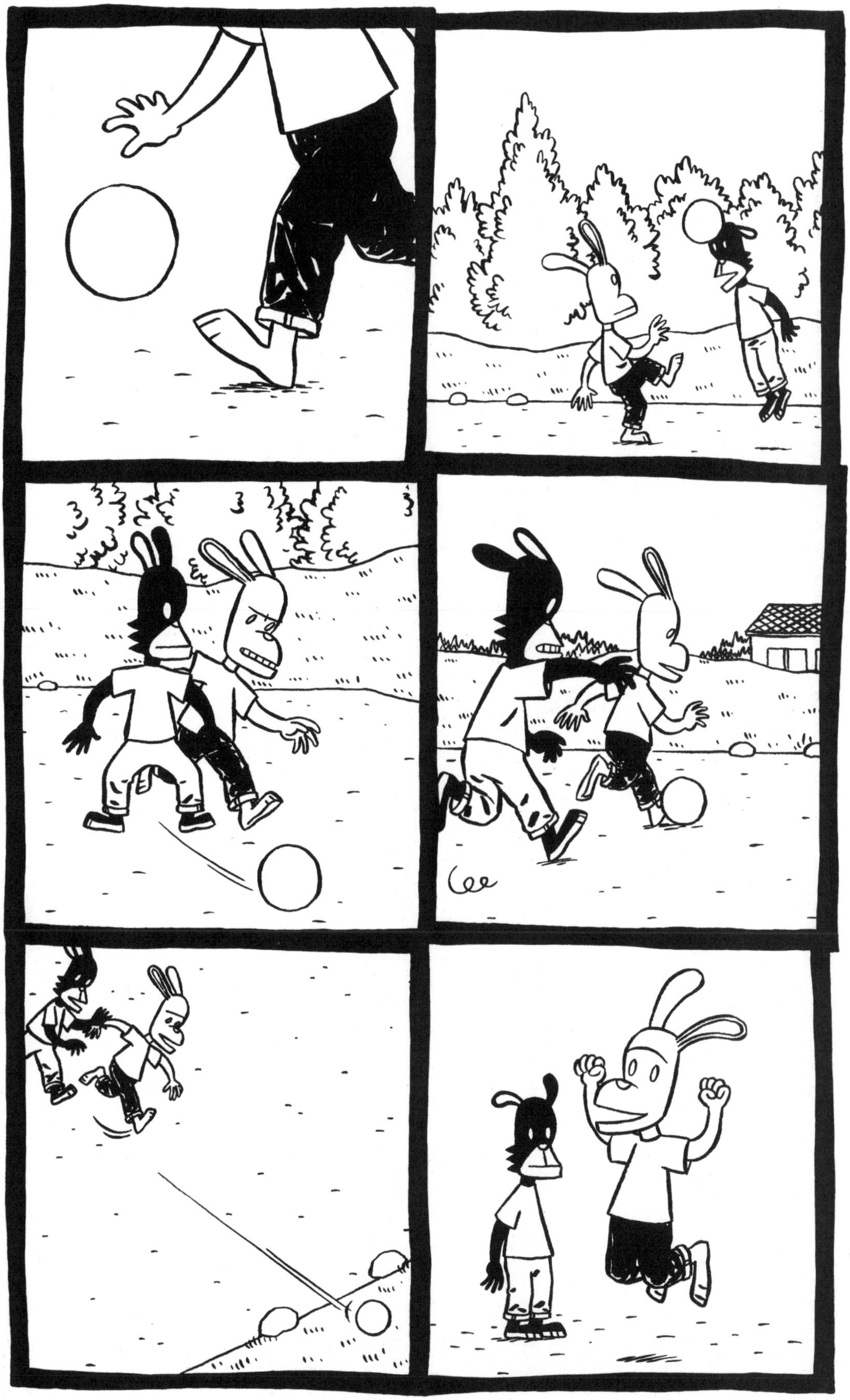

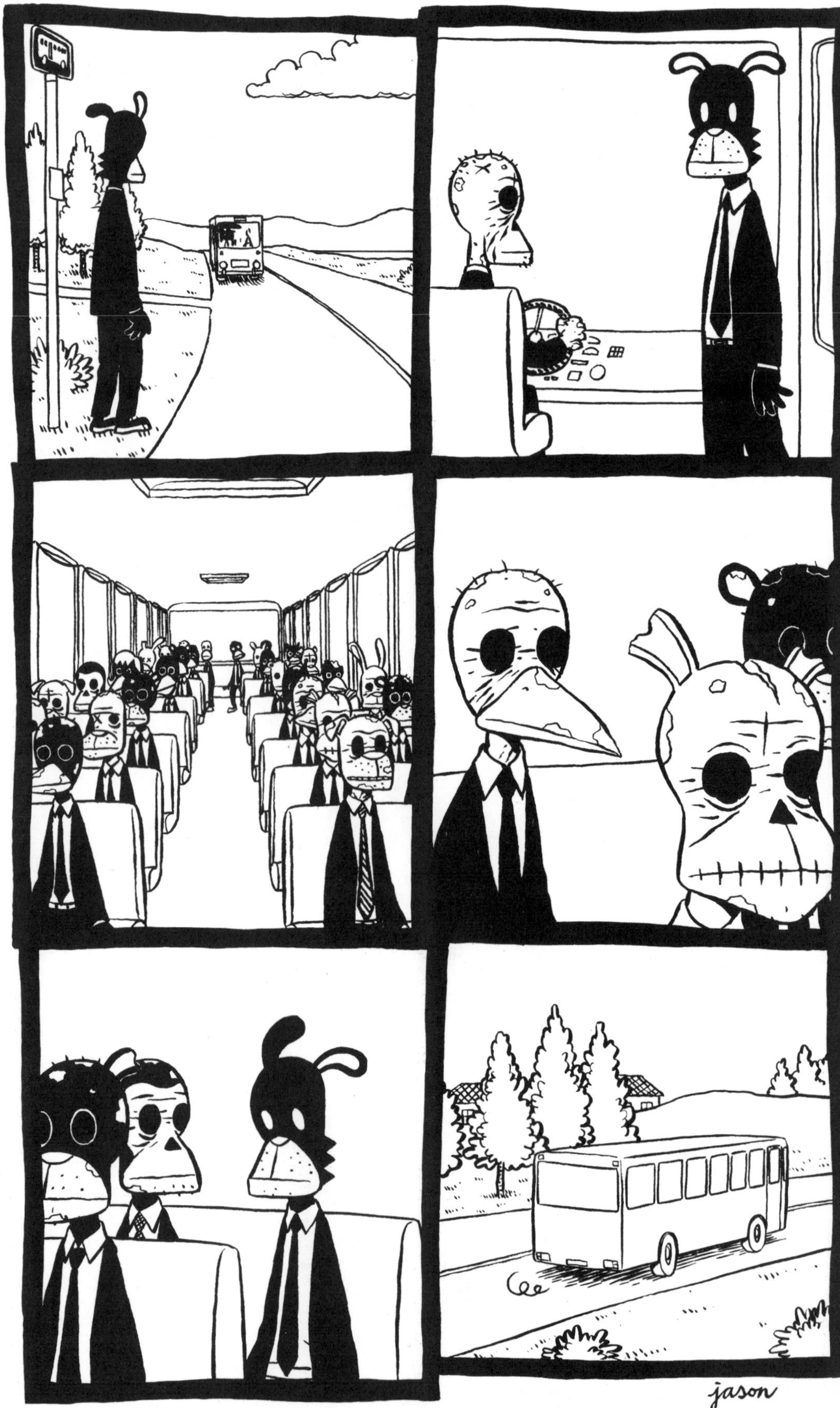
jason